Praise for *A Body to Love*

"*A Body to Love* is a powerful and most important thing we humans ability to connect with our authentic selves and with others. Angie has a way of communicating her truth in a way that's vulnerable, authentic, soothing, safe, and empowering. As always, I'm blown away by Angie's writing, and I am positive that *A Body to Love* will move so many."

> —**NATALIE ROSE ALLEN**, MPsy, RP, creator
> of wakeupandsmelltherosay.

"This book is a powerful and moving—too many will be able to relate to it. Angie's warm voice feels like hearing from a best friend who is sharing the most sticky vulnerable parts of herself, and it encourages you to feel comfortable to share yours too. This book not only acknowledges the harm of media and marketing on our relationship with food and our bodies, it also provides reflective tools and prompts to challenge them. Recovering from diet culture and disordered eating can feel like a lonely, isolating journey. Angie's warmth and vulnerability remind readers that they are not alone and that recovery is possible. Anyone who has ever had a 'complicated' relationship with food or their body will benefit from this book."

> —**BRENNA O'MALLEY**, registered dietitian and
> founder of The Wellful

a body
TO
love

a body

TO

Cultivate Community, Body Positivity, and Self-Love in the Age of Social Media

By **Angelina Caruso**

mango
PUBLISHING

CORAL GABLES

Copyright © 2021 by Angelina Caruso.
Published by Mango Publishing, a division of Mango Publishing Group, Inc.

Cover & Layout Design: Carmen Fortunato
Cover Art: AdobeStock

Mango is an active supporter of authors' rights to free speech and artistic expression in their books. The purpose of copyright is to encourage authors to produce exceptional works that enrich our culture and our open society.

Uploading or distributing photos, scans or any content from this book without prior permission is theft of the author's intellectual property. Please honor the author's work as you would your own. Thank you in advance for respecting our author's rights.

For permission requests, please contact the publisher at:
Mango Publishing Group
2850 S Douglas Road, 2nd Floor
Coral Gables, FL 33134 USA
info@mango.bz

For special orders, quantity sales, course adoptions and corporate sales, please email the publisher at sales@mango.bz. For trade and wholesale sales, please contact Ingram Publisher Services at customer.service@ingramcontent.com or +1.800.509.4887.

A Body to Love: Cultivate Community, Body Positivity, and Self-Love in the Age of Social Media

Library of Congress Cataloging-in-Publication number: 2021942076
ISBN: (print) 978-1-64250-685-3, (ebook) 978-1-64250-686-0
BISAC category code SEL014000, SELF-HELP / Eating Disorders & Body Image

To my bodies: past, present, and future.
I'm sorry, thank you, and I'm excited to meet you.

Contents

PART II: AFTER SOCIAL MEDIA

Foreword

There is something incredible about recovering from an eating disorder; it's near impossible to put into words. The thing is, Angie is incredible with words. She can encapsulate the essence of freedom from an eating disorder. She has taken the struggles and heartaches from her battle and turned them into a uniquely beautiful story.

You will read Angie's story throughout *A Body to Love*, how she has been able to heal through her triumphs and pitfalls. This is a unique lens of a journey that now, hundreds of thousands have been able to engage with through social media. Her talent is so apparent through these lessons as she teaches you how to be a conscious consumer by avoiding negative aspects of social media, which is so utterly important in the modern era of technology.

As an eating disorder registered dietitian, I met Angie through the social media community she has curated. We became quick friends with similar interests and a mutual sarcastic sense of humor. We have laughed and cried through it all, connecting on both sides of recovery, the healer and the healing.

You can never win your eating disorder, but you can win recovery.

Sarah Chau, MS, RDN

Introduction

Before You Read

What follows is the story of when, for some time, I stopped living and feeling. And how I found my way back.

My relationship with my emotions has never been neutral. I've either felt deeply and forcefully, or not at all, in denial, in fear, on a mission to repress and pretend.

Hardship has not hardened me; rather, it has softened my edges. Trauma has shown me the power in vulnerability, in surrendering. Why do we wage battle against ourselves? For what purpose? I led a years-long war attacking myself. I grew exhausted. Hating my body was my full-time job. Everywhere I turned, I couldn't escape from my physical form. I believed my body was my enemy.

For years, I starved myself and exercised into oblivion. I harbored a desperate desire to shrink, to go unnoticed, and yet, I wanted to be the best. I wanted praise. I wanted others to notice that I was "disciplined" or "dedicated" or "the healthiest." I grew obsessed with how I looked and what I ate because I believed these aspects spoke to my worth as a person. This is what I learned from society at large, and more specifically, from my use of social media as a young teenager. I turned to strangers online to define health for me. I scrolled through diet plans and photos of bodies in bathing suits and workout videos, and I felt an unbearable pressure to conform. I made myself sick over this.

Eating disorders are contradictions. They are mental chaos, paradoxes, lives lived in the absence of logic and rationality. I wanted polar opposites at all times. I wanted to be forgotten, and yet I wanted to be idolized. In the deepest trenches of my illness, I despised the body that carried me through my days, not because it was taking up too much space, but because whatever space it was taking up was never good enough. I knew I was unwell. I knew it when I saw stars while trekking up a staircase. I knew it when I slid into the hard plastic seat of a desk in a high school classroom and an electric pain would shoot up my tailbone, spreading like wildfire through my body. I knew it when I would throw my lunch away before heading to my first-period class, or when my childhood clothes would fall off my teenage body into puddles of despair at my feet.

My eating disorder revealed again and again how rapidly I was approaching a fatal end. A slow heartbeat. Hunger pains rattled, a constant hum and an occasional pang. Everything about the body I saw, the body I owned, I hated. This is how my eating disorder began.

And this is how it ended.

Because I had finally had enough.

When I began healing the wounds of my eating disorder, I was told I was in "recovery." I was taught that this word defines the journey of moving from sick to healed. That a person in recovery is still in the midst of their illness, deeply buried in the thing that plagues them. That they are in a stage where they can rationally acknowledge the presence of this thing and are working to mend this thing, but they are *not yet rid* of this thing. Yet. And that is the goal we're taught to understand; that this journey is finished when that thing is unlearned, forgotten, stripped out of the very veins it once ran violently through. Forgotten from the brain it once controlled.

Who decided that this is what recovery is? This definition works for physical ailments and injuries; for the wrongs we can see, the ones that are tangible. We break our arm and then recover, and there is an end goal, a destination. The injury is healed.

In my opinion, as humans, we are sometimes threatened by what we cannot see, by what we cannot hold and analyze with our senses. We feel threatened by mental illness because there is no singular or universal understanding of the mind. These ailments are subjective and contextual, and complicated, and agonizing. We want so desperately to believe that we can rid someone of a mental illness in the same clean-cut way we can a physical injury. Many believe that a person is in recovery, and then they are not. There is a start and a finish. A before and after.

But what if recovery is not a journey to a final destination, but simply just a journey to something new, something more, something healthier? To a place where the illness fails to *prevail*. The voice isn't forgotten. It isn't unlearned. But the person in recovery can learn to speak over it. Recovery speaks in daily choices, in narratives, in perspectives, in beliefs, and in practices that we consciously make for ourselves.

Recovery from a mental illness is not losing that illness.

It's gaining the courage to face it and do something about it.

Struggles that aren't observable on the outside can isolate us. Whether it's an eating disorder, body dysmorphia, or simply feelings of low self-confidence, issues that eat us up on the inside are hard to detect. It leads to isolation. We can't always tell that people around us may, like us, be dealing with pain. How comforting would it be to know that those toxic thoughts in your mind aren't yours alone, but something to which thousands of others can relate?

What a breath of fresh air it would be to express your deepest pains and be reassured by others that you're not alone; that they are with you and are rooting for you.

Recovery is an intimidating journey. It calls on the person in recovery to dive deeply into a place of discomfort. It often feels like a task we must take on alone. This, for me at least, was why I faced countless relapses in my eating disorder; I felt misunderstood by those around me. I didn't believe anyone in my life could understand the turmoil I felt inside. What saved me was a community of people who *did* understand, who *did* empathize on the deepest level. A community that took these dark, twisted, taboo topics and shone such a bright light on them I couldn't look away.

Community saved me. Community is the greatest gift I can give you, regardless of your specific past and traumas. Whatever it is you struggle with, I promise you're not alone.

I've found that writing helps me express myself, so this book focuses heavily on the act of writing. I mentioned before that connection with others was, and continues to be, a significant factor in my healing process, and I hope it will be for you, too.

Before I was able to connect with others, I had to connect with myself. Writing helped me understand my deepest heart. When I was sick, I lived in constant fear and paranoia, numbing my true desires and emotions to clear headspace used for fixating on food and exercise. I had forgotten who I was. I had misplaced my character and my soul. I saw myself as my eating disorder, and my eating disorder as me, and we were one, and who was *I*, really?

When I finally began a real recovery process, I wrote every single day. I kept a journal. I wrote in all caps when I was frustrated with my changing body. I wrote with an excessive number of commas when my thoughts were racing after a scary meal. I forced myself to write when I wanted to the least because I knew the cathartic rush that came from putting my feelings into words on paper was what I needed the most.

At the time, my feelings and fears were wound up within each other, and I couldn't see them clearly. I was overwhelmed. I didn't know where to start or how to make any progress. The act of writing was the act of undoing the knots, one by one, for me, and I hope it will be for you as well.

That is why, throughout this book, you'll be asked to write and open yourself up. You'll find plenty of guiding questions and mantras for you to contemplate. There are no rules to writing; write what is there, on the tip of your tongue, what is bursting at the seams of your skin.

I spent years hating myself, and then I wrote, and I wrote, and I wrote, and I met myself all over again, and it was someone I liked. Community and connection are vital to our lives, but we cannot wholly connect with others if we are distant from ourselves. Knowing who we are inside is critical for both cultivating a strong community and getting the most we can out of it.

We may not always understand why we feel the way we do or why we choose to behave the way we do, but simply attempting to make sense of it through words can help us see with greater clarity. Writing brought me to myself. I brought myself to a community. There are stages to this epic, forever-in-flux process of growing, but we can't embark on it until we begin to unearth our truest selves.

You don't have to be a writer to be a writer. We are all writers. We all experience feeling lost and confused at times, and words can help us find our way.

Once I began unearthing my truest self and unraveling the disordered voice from my healthy one, I found myself contributing to and reaping benefits from an unexpected community.

In the initial weeks of my commitment to a real recovery, I found myself on Instagram. Out of curiosity, I poked around the hashtags for peaks into recovery. I didn't expect to find much as I typed in *#EatingDisorderRecovery*, but I was floored when hundreds of posts come up from men and women in my very circumstances, providing glimpses into this grueling, terrifying, incomprehensible phenomenon that is healing from a mental illness. Here were people, *real* people in *real* time, reassuring me that I wasn't alone in this journey.

For weeks, I ghost followed these accounts—meaning I never connected with them but turned to them at all hours of the day. I watched as these people supported each other in moments of paralyzing fear or in instances of self-doubt, debating whether the discomfort of recovery was worth it in the end or not—spoiler, it is!

Eventually, I bit the bullet and created a recovery account for my journey. Like those who inspired me, I planned to use this tool to hold myself accountable for meeting my meal plan.

I was self-conscious about keeping this diary, so I made sure there were no ties to my real life. There were no photos of me, and I never used my real name.

When it came time to title this account, I asked myself one question: *What am I looking to gain here?* The answer came simply, softly. It just made sense. I was in pursuit of strength. I was @seekingstrongerwings.

I shared photos to my feed six times a day: three snacks, three meals. For some reason, I felt that if I shared that I was eating a meal for breakfast and two people saw it, then I simply *had* to follow through with complying. I would indicate in my captions that I was afraid of this food or that snack, and the comments that were posted would encourage me to stay strong. Strangers were taking the time out of their days to simply send a kind message my way. To lift me up when I felt I couldn't carry on. To show me that life in and after recovery is worth fighting for. These strangers kept me from falling back into yet another relapse. They were the support I needed to keep fighting. People who understood my pain, my fears, my deepest, darkest desires. I was finally, *finally* able to stay true to recovery because I had something I never had in the past: support from people who have experienced what I've been through and made it out alive.

Keeping a photo-based food diary meant I spent a lot of time looking at and taking pictures of food, which allowed me to focus on food in a new, healthier way. As time trickled on and I began to heal, I found myself excited to cook and create in the kitchen. I wanted to try new foods and develop recipes and share my newfound love for these practices. I spent years crying over food, and now I was eager to explore the beautiful world of nourishment. It was an incredibly significant shift for me. I was proud. I wanted to own my creations. So, I took another important step: I added my name to my profile and changed my blank profile photo to one of my face. I was ready to both show the world how far I've come and to take them with me on my ever-continuing adventure.

I was no longer in initial recovery anymore. A few years removed from this stage in my life, I was now maintaining my health. I was college-bound, leaving home for the first time. I was learning from those I connected with how exciting food can be. I was beginning to understand food's ability to heal us and help us feel our best. My account captured these elements of my life, and my content became a mix of lifestyle with a heavy focus on health, wellness, and open discussions on recovery.

I never set out with the goal of becoming an "influencer" or in hopes of cultivating a large following. I was a girl in pain. I was scared. I was dying. I turned to social media for support. Everything that came after was by chance and fate, a product of community and relationships. I wrote, and I began to tap into my truest self. I took this self to a community and was able to connect with others thanks to this newfound introspection.

This journey has led me from @seekingstrongerwings to @healthfulradiance. It is my little corner of the internet where I am living deeply, freely, and authentically. It is a space where I am open and vulnerable. It is where my truth goes to be exposed and where people from all walks of life can find light and hope in the hustle and bustle of their day. My goal with this platform is to prove my eating disorder wrong every single day. My eating disorder swore I would always be miserable. That I'd never find happiness, or stability, or joy. That I would die young. That I could never help others because I could never even help myself.

I found this place where I could change my narrative.

I'm writing this book because I wish it existed when I was sick and dying from an eating disorder. I wish I could have read it and understood that the unhealthy patterns, thoughts, and behaviors I was falling into were red flags. I wish I could have read this book before these elements turned into an eating disorder at all. I wish I could have flipped through it and found words for the pain I struggled to comprehend, the discomfort I felt when I looked in the mirror. The struggle of obsessing over my body. The burnout from worrying about how I looked in my clothes or what others thought when they saw me in a bathing suit. I wish I could have bought copies for my parents and my sisters and everyone in my life, so they could understand, truly, what it's like to struggle with disordered relationships with food and with body image, and how quickly and quietly they can turn into something much, much worse.

However, I want to truly drive home the point that I can only speak from my personal experience. This book is what *I* know an eating disorder to be. I struggled with anorexia, with exercise addiction. I can't speak to binge eating, or bulimia, or EDNOS, for example. I won't bend what I know and apply it to these struggles; however, my goal is to help people struggling with *any* issue, whether an eating disorder, mental illness, or something else. I want people to know that no matter what hurt they are experiencing, there is a community for them. I want to show them how to find people who care. I've chosen to open my heart in hopes that you can find comfort and light in the words I share.

I must stress the importance of being a conscious consumer. My story is vulnerable, utterly honest, transparent, and uncensored. While I refuse to include unnecessary details such as weights and calories, I discuss triggering behaviors and irrational lines of thinking. I wouldn't communicate my pain and suffering if I were to censor my past entirely. This is my history, and every day I work toward owning it. If you are questioning whether or not reading this book is a good idea, hold off. It'll be here when you're ready. Respect where you are in your journey. Pass this book to a loved one, a friend, someone in your life who can be there for you. It may help them understand what you need during this time.

This book is written from a place of consistent health and happiness. I refuse to call myself "recovered," as this feels finite to me, as if my eating disorder is forgotten. I don't believe this is possible. I believe I'll know my eating disorder for the rest of my life because it will always live within me. What separates my past self from my present one is a resilience I call upon daily. The recovery process is forever, but eventually, it is simply a part of life, not life itself.

Whatever it was that drew you to this book, I'm happy to have you here. I hope that by sharing my story and exposing the unexpectedly brilliant and beautiful side of social media, we can open a conversation about eating disorders that is honest, empowering, and comfortable.

To the people who never left my side, thank you. To those who let me breathe, thank you.

To the online community that saved my life, the very same one to which I strive to give back every day, thank you so very much.

Part I:

Before Social Media

Chapter 1

Bad Information

One Size Does Not Fit All

After dinner on Easter Sunday, the year my eating disorder began, my mom cleared the table for the dessert spread. My stomach was already bloated, stretching the band of my skirt, and I couldn't see my toes, but it was time to dig in. Three of these, two of those, a couple of glasses of milk. My sister offered to make hot chocolate for everyone. I couldn't resist.

I made my way up to my room that night and looked in the mirror before getting ready for bed. I couldn't look away. My tummy was protruding out what felt like yards. I laid my body across my bed to alleviate the stomachache parading through my midsection. It disturbed me, how large I suddenly looked. Why did I eat so much? For the first time in my life, I felt angry at myself for eating.

On that day, I swore to go on a "diet." I had only ever heard the word tossed around before on TV shows and magazine headlines, but it felt right at that moment.

I wasn't exactly sure how to start. Everything I knew about "health" I had learned from mass media. Advertisements for juice cleanses and workout programs came to mind. I began by fixating on a body part that I wasn't happy with and set out to avenge it. For me, this manifested as a need for a "flat stomach."

My first Google search of this journey was "how to get a flat tummy."

I was a girl on a mission.

I had been taught exercise leads to weight loss, which leads to health. So, I began there with treadmill runs. It wasn't long before this new diet-focused pursuit trickled into my daily intake. Running was only half the equation. "Abs are made in the kitchen," I read somewhere. Probably some online fitness forum.

Without proper *media literacy* skills, these online forums and message boards seemed so appealing to me. Media literacy refers to one's ability to interact with media in an informed and conscious way. (We'll go into detail about it in Part II.) But for now, keep this in mind: media literacy means multiple gears are turning in your brain as you take in messages. It's being mindful of the author's authority (or lack of authority) on the subject and their intention in spreading the message.

The day I decided to go on a "diet," I was young, vulnerable, and impressionable. It didn't even cross my mind that there were sites on the internet that had their agenda in mind, not my agenda, and that they may be feeding me false messages. I didn't stop to think about who these people were or wonder whether their advice was sound. I read mantras like, "Nothing tastes as good as skinny feels," with a photo of a photoshopped model in a bikini below it, and I thought about it for days on end.

I look back and wish I could have sounded the alarms, sent them blaring through my childhood bedroom. *Don't do that! What you're seeing is just one day out of many ordinary days.* That day, I decided to stand in front of the mirror after a full day of holiday eats and judge my body.

If you take anything away from the above, let it be the idea that there is no such thing as one size fits all. Body image is a topic every person on earth has a relationship with, especially since we all view our bodies through a certain lens. How many times have you judged and shamed your body based on how it compares to someone else's? It's time to stop. It's incredibly easy to criticize our bodies and internalize social pressures. Our bodies change and grow throughout our lives. Embrace the beauty in this ebb and flow.

. . . .

Understanding health as a concept that feels different for every individual has been instrumental to my healing and how I interact with media now. Below are some questions you can ask yourself to strengthen your media literacy muscles, specifically in social media spaces.

PRODUCER: Who is writing/sharing this message?

▶ Is this person an expert on the topic they're writing about?

▶ Is this simply someone sharing their personal experience?

*Note: Be mindful of what is an opinion and what is a fact before you take anything to heart.

INTENTION: What is the intention behind this message/ad/post?

⏵ Is it sponsored by a brand or service?

⏵ Does this person truly believe that this product will guarantee you a certain result, or are they paid to spread a positive message regarding it?

*Note: These situations may not always be disclosed clearly, so make sure to remember that not everything you see or read is the genuine truth.

IMPACT: Does the content you are interacting with genuinely make you feel good?

⏵ If something feels wrong or disturbs you somehow, remember that you have the power to choose the content you consume.

⏵ Be a conscious consumer. (More on this in Part II.)

⏵ Mute accounts and platforms that don't serve you.

⏵ Unfollow.

⏵ Block.

⏵ Restrict.

⏵ If there are messages out there hindering your positive self-growth, they can be arguably fatal. Protect yourself and your well-being.

Fixation Isn't Dedication

When we fixate on little things, they grow, often becoming larger-than-life, with larger than-life-consequences. We can forget that in the grand scheme of our lives, the temporary object of our fixation has virtually no impact at all.

The summer I started to lose weight, I felt there was always more I could do, more progress to achieve. Each day, I challenged myself to run another few blocks. I moved from bread to rice cakes, from peanut butter to peanut powder. I grew convinced I didn't *need* the "extra" food. It would just sit on my stomach. I had worked too hard to risk *that*.

This is what held my focus daily. Food, food, food. Everything was food-focused, and I had come to consider food a threat. I thought about how to avoid it and how to have less of it. How to make excuses for not needing any at all. How to justify my food resistance to those around me.

I fixated on every bite of food I ate. I made up food rules and embraced food-related personal values. I had come to idealize nutritional ideals that were not only untrue and unhealthy, but they were also outrageous. They became my core values that formed my beliefs about food and health, and with these as my foundation, it was inevitable that my life became colored by constant food and body-focused paranoia.

Looking back, I can recall many times when I believed my obsessive fixation was an innocent dedication to my health and well-being. In late August, I tried out for my high school's freshman volleyball team. There was a week-long training camp before tryouts, and I spent hours each day melting in a stuffy gymnasium, running laps, and peppering the volleyball until my forearms were bloodshot and not even four rounds of Icy Hot helped. I loved every second.

When we made the team, my best friend and I celebrated with lunch at Panera, and I allowed myself a few bites of a brownie—one of the thick frosted ones that sat at the register. These few bites became all I could focus on for the next three days. *Why did I do that?* I was still fixating on those bites as I stood in the shower before bed. I didn't sleep that night or the next. My skin felt tight.

This fixation was taxing. It made me restless. For three bites of a brownie to fully occupy my thoughts for seventy-two hours was not tied to logic. My relationship with food was taking up my entire day, my entire life.

Years later, I recognize these harmful core values. Recognition and self-awareness are key in healing toxic thought cycles and changing one's social media focus from "diet help" to restorative healing communities.

If you find yourself having a similar fixation experience, I suggest you acknowledge your feelings and identify their toxicity. Be mindful of *why* you are feeling the way you are and intentionally check the accuracy of your beliefs—whether you have incorrect conceptions about food or other issues you are struggling with, turn your attention to what is healthy for you as an individual.

Everything you need to heal is within you, even if you don't realize it quite yet. Pay attention to your thoughts and call yourself out on lies you are buying into. Note any obsessions you are having. Toxic beliefs need to be vanquished from your mindset.

In this situation, some of my core values were ones I internalized after years of consuming the diet/fitness industry's content at large.

Here are some untruths I was fixated on:

▶ Food is either "good" or "bad," and I cannot consume anything "bad" without instantly gaining weight, which means I have failed.

▶ Resisting foods that tempt me makes me strong, while indulging in them makes me weak.

▶ The only way to redeem myself from "giving in" is forcing myself to "make up for it."

Note some unhealthy untruths you may be fixating on:

_____

_____

_____

_____

Now make a new list right below it, one that outlines truthful replacements for each one. Here is mine:

▶ All food is welcome. I open my heart to nourishing both my body and my soul.

▶ Fueling my body to simply *live* and *stay alive* is an act of self-care. Failing to maintain my life is not admirable by any means.

❱ Food does not have power over me. When I accept this, I don't feel "tempted" by foods I "can't have." In the absence of such pressure, I can breathe.

_____

_____

_____

_____

_____

_____

_____

_____

Writing out these mantras gives me something tangible to look at and read back to myself when I feel vulnerable or need to redirect my focus onto a healthy relationship with food. I read the words out loud and hear the toxicity of the lies I used to believe. I then shift my focus to my new, healthy core values. It may not make the toxic thoughts go away, but intentionally shifting my focus helps me understand why I'm feeling this way.

Chapter 2

Sinking Deeper

Lying to Others

Since I can't go back in time and call myself out then, I'll do the next best thing: help you call yourself out now.

I'm not suggesting you expose your lies to anyone just yet, but acknowledging them, facing them, and owning them yourself is a pivotal first step.

All I ever did was lie.

I lied about everything under the sun, about anything that would threaten my eating disorder's ability to flourish. I lied to everyone in my life. I lied to myself.

This manipulative behavior had deep, long-lasting consequences. When I lied and was caught, I diminished the trust I had established with that person. Trust is a deeply valuable asset in a relationship. What is a relationship without trust, anyway? It is, honestly, a waste of time.

Most of the relationships in my life fell apart because of this disintegration of trust.

My coach didn't trust me, so she let me go.

Later, my teachers, friends, doctors, and sisters all lost trust in me, lost faith in me, and finally, all made the gut-wrenching decisions to let me go as well.

I knew I was lying. I knew exactly what I was doing. Looking back, it should have bothered me more. But I never let myself think about the damage I was doing. Don't get me wrong: I knew what I was doing was wrong and harmful. But at the time, I shut down, shut it out, and pretended it wasn't happening.

The foundation of love is trust, both when it comes to loving yourself and when it comes to having relationships with those around you. How can you love yourself if you don't believe you are worthy of the truth? How can you be at peace when you're suppressing your body and mind's messages to you? The longer you spend living in lies, the further from yourself you'll grow, and the more you lie to those around you, the more difficult it is to be in healthy relationships with them.

. . . .

I can tell you that ignorance is not bliss. Not here.

For a long time, I wasn't brave enough to stop lying because lying felt safe, even if I knew it was wrong.

Take a moment to bring forth the innermost thoughts that you may know, deep down, are not accurate—even if you don't want to face that fact yet. Write them here. Write down the false beliefs you've grown attached to and put them on the page. Writing helps bring them into the light. The lies become visible—real. And once they are real, you can work toward finding your way out of the web of untruths you've been both telling yourself and others. Acknowledge them. It's a healthy step toward gaining control of them. They will no longer control you.

Cool, right?

Take a few minutes to dive into this exercise. A table is always a fun time, isn't it? I'm a visual learner; you might be too. Either way, there's some writing involved as per usual.

Write what comes to mind. If it feels wrong and you are afraid to put words to that thought, *excellent.* Those are the ones we're looking for here. Let them out. Be honest here. Lying in an exercise about lying just flat out defeats the purpose.

Who you might be lying to	What the lie is	What the truth is	Why you're lying

Once you complete this chart, step away from it for a few minutes. Return to it when you are ready to analyze what's in front of you, what you've been neglecting to do something about. Hopefully, this gives you a little wake-up call. When I filled this chart out recently, acknowledging all the lies I have told broke my heart. But heartbreak can heal us.

. . . .

Lying to Yourself

When my freshman year of high school ended, I didn't do much with my summer. I was chronically tired and cranky. The mood swings were terrifying. I snapped constantly, violently. My friends stopped reaching out. I had shut nearly everyone out.

Was this what I wanted?

I'm not sure what I wanted. At the time, I had convinced myself that I wanted to be "healthy," but I never stopped to think about what that meant. I knew there was a disconnect there but never really exposed it for what it was.

By this point, I had lost too much weight. My parents could barely look at me without having to leave the room. I had maxed out on my exercise addiction. I became lethargic and always empty. I reasoned that if I ate less, I didn't even have to work out. So that's the route I took.

Sometimes, when we allow misinformation to form into our belief system, our judgment is impaired. The more time we spend with these beliefs, the more inclined we are to hold them as true, even if they're not.

I started thinking irrationally because I grew attached to losing weight, a feat I believed was a testament to my strength of character. I grew attached to the rules I had made up that allowed me to succeed in this pursuit. I grew attached to photos and workouts and meal plans I saw online—all promising thinness and happiness as if the two are inexorably tied together. I truly believed they were. I trusted the voice in my head and blindly obeyed every demand—even the grossly irrational ones. I couldn't fathom that these practices and mindsets were hurting me. I truly couldn't see it.

How had it gotten so bad? At what point had I surrendered control of my thoughts and the safety of my headspace to a voice that wasn't mine?

Have you ever lost sight of yourself when faced with so much external noise? How irrational it is to scroll for hours online? How irrational it is to idolize one body type? You may be filling your days with the lives of other people: what they eat, how they move, the reflections they see in their mirrors. The more time you spend consuming *their* lives, the less time you're investing in *your* health and happiness. Your relationship with food and your body is uniquely yours. You don't need to force yourself to adopt the practices you see others following. You don't have to lie and convince yourself that you're someone you're not. Your needs are simply different than someone else's. They're not better, nor worse.

Call to mind someone you love and care about deeply, someone for whom you want only the best. You would never dream of steering this person wrong or hurting them. I always think of my little sisters.

Now that you have this person in mind, I want you to pretend you're having a conversation with them. Outline for them the harmful practices you live by, and then encourage them to do the same. My irrationality was food-related, so my list is as well. For this exercise, tailor your notes to reflect your circumstances.

- **Don't** eat when you're hungry
- **Don't** "give in" to bodily cues telling you to eat
- **Do** fixate over and judge your body
- **Do** speak to yourself negatively or with a hateful heart

I would never want my sisters to live this way. Writing out those lines of thinking and picturing my sisters following each mantra helps me see the irrationality I was living by with crystal clarity.

Now, let's fix up those tragic rules above (and the tragic rules that may be dictating your life). For me, it's:

- **Do** eat when you're hungry
- **Do** honor your body's hunger cues
- **Don't** waste time fixating over and judging your body
- **Don't** speak to yourself negatively or with a hateful heart

What do all these statements have in common? They promote a healthy and strong relationship with *oneself*. These rules bring to light an established self-trust, which we depend on to keep ourselves alive and well. What are your statements telling you?

Most importantly, we should never punish ourselves for having the same needs we'd encourage others to nourish. There is balance; there is equality.

As you focus on this exercise for yourself, take the original set of rules you write and then edit them to account for logic, reason, compassion, and self-respect. The shift will be simple, a few words maybe. But the weight each statement carries will change drastically.

Chapter 3

Denial

Your Worth Is Not Conditional

My mother told me she was taking me to my annual eye exam, and I believed her.

But instead of heading in the direction I expected, she hooked a sharp right into the parking lot of the local hospital, and a wave of panic rushed over me. The fear made me feel like I was drowning. She said nothing, yet I knew.

My mom cut the engine but didn't get out. She wouldn't look at me.

"I've been talking to a doctor here for a few weeks," she told me. "He specializes in eating disorders, and—" she choked. She looked through the windshield, unable to meet my eyes. I realized she had never said the words out loud before.

Eating disorders.

Twenty minutes later, I was in a small room in the hospital's eating disorders unit. The doctor entered, and our examination began and ended with one glance, up and down. The doctor turned to my mom and spoke. He sounded bored, disappointed almost, as if my situation didn't challenge him.

"Oh, she's anorexic, all right."

That day was the first time I was attached to a diagnosis. I wasn't sure how to feel. A label provided a sense of clarity, but at the same time, nothing felt different. I already knew my relationships with food and my body were damaged. I already knew that it wasn't natural for me to feel nervous in anticipation of meals or to feel anxiety when I passed my reflection. I already knew that I was trapped in a cycle of toxic thoughts and behaviors. I had just been denying it. Lying. Simply telling myself that this was the cost of being "healthy."

Not everyone reading this book will relate to having a diagnosed eating disorder, but no matter what you are struggling with, I hope that you too will find help in the exercises in this book and will find a healing community that gives you the support you need.

And please know that there is no such thing as having to be sick enough. If you are living in a way that is hurting you, interfering with your ability to be happy and healthy, then *that* is more than enough of a reason to seek help. We do not need to validate our choices when making ones that will improve our mental well-being. We do not need to lie to ourselves to appear strong to those around us. There is strength in vulnerability and acceptance.

I went on to see a few more specialists, general MDs, psychiatrists, and therapists, and all arrived at the same conclusion. I encountered many ways of being diagnosed—

some asked questions, some charted my weight over short periods, and others ran extensive tests, but all concurred.

Interestingly, although I ultimately worked with many specialists, it wasn't until I found a community through social media that my healing process began. Social media can be damaging, but it also can be healing and revitalizing if you find a safe online community of support. I discuss how to do that in Part II, but for now, know that others are going through the same thing. You may not see your struggles and pains out in the world around you—this is why online communities are so influential on a healing journey. You can find others who truly understand your struggles, people who get it, and who are rooting for you.

- -

Here's a narrative you've probably convinced yourself of before:

"When I'm _____ enough, I'll _____."

Here's an example: When I'm thin enough, I'll be happy.

Another one: When I'm sick enough, I'll be worthy of help.

This conditional way of thinking forces us to rely on external factors to validate our worth. Have you ever framed your outlook on life in this way? See if you can fill in the following blanks with past or present beliefs.

When I'm _____ , I'll _____ .

When I'm _____ , I'll _____ .

When I'm _____ , I'll _____ .

Now read those back to yourself. Read them out loud, just to hear how false they are. Our happiness and worth are beautifully complex concepts and are therefore contingent on thousands of little things. There is so much that collectively makes up each, and to fixate on one specific factor is exhausting.

Acknowledge Your Fears

Believe it or not, fear is what saved my life. Although my eating disorder was destructive, it had become my comfort zone—and being taken out of my comfort zone was terrifying. But the fear I experienced when I was taken to the hospital was my first step toward healing.

What I've since come to understand is there are different kinds of fear. Some fear is a healthy response to a harmful situation. Other fear is destructive—such as being afraid to eat.

When the doctor suggested I be admitted, "overwhelmed" wasn't a big enough word to capture my feelings.

My mind was spinning: *They're going to feed you. They're going to stop you from exercising. You're going to be so unhealthy. How can you live with yourself? All your hard work, for nothing.*

I talked my way into being an outpatient by agreeing to everything they wanted me to do. Half an hour later, I was seated at the kitchen table at home. My mom slid a plastic plate in front of me. A sandwich. My body reacted before my mind, and I felt my mouth slightly salivate. A fleeting thought passed—*that looks so good*—and I was ashamed. When did I become so weak? I believed that having bodily needs was a weakness and that honoring them only fueled this weakness further.

Despite this, I took a bite.

I took another bite. And another. I didn't look up. I was terrified that moving my head even the slightest degree would trigger the voice, and I would have to stop eating. I didn't want to; I didn't want to stop until the hunger pains were laid to rest.

But those hunger pains weren't gone after one sandwich. I had to keep pushing. Even when it was scary. Even when it felt wrong. Even when each bite plummeted to the bottom of my stomach and burst into a thousand flames of fear.

Fear about my body image began my descent into a full-fledged eating disorder. And the fear of dying is what ultimately helped me begin my journey back to health. Pay attention to what makes you afraid. Really analyze it and notice whether it's healthy fear or unhealthy fear.

At that moment, my disorder manifested into fear of simply eating a sandwich. It was terrifying. Of course, this looks different to all of us. Does fear arise when you look in the mirror? Maybe it arises when you take a selfie. Do you feel fear when you wear a certain article of clothing? No matter when you are feeling fear, it is important you acknowledge it and analyze why you are afraid. Body positivity starts when you prioritize how you feel on the inside over what you can see on the outside. Your health and wellness are felt, not seen.

Broken relationships with ourselves can disturb natural, healthy brain functions—we are failing to fuel our bodies and brains in the right ways, and our internal processes suffer. Our job is to avoid this from happening by identifying our irrational fears as exactly that, irrational.

What are you afraid of that isn't an immediate threat to your safety? Write it down:

_____

_____

_____

_____

_____

_____

_____

_____

_____

_____

_____

_____

The next time you're faced with that irrational fear, what actions can you take? Could you lean on a trusted friend or family member to talk through it? For me, it might be planning an activity with a friend when I'm feeling forced to work out. We each have our own struggles, but take a few minutes to think through what might help you when you are faced with irrational fear.

_____

_____

_____

_____

_____

_____

_____

_____

_____

_____

_____

Chapter 4

Ebbs and Flows

Building a Community with Yourself

Weeks went by, and they all looked the same. I was desperate to connect with someone who understood my exhaustion. I needed encouragement. From what I could tell, my peers weren't afraid of food. They didn't feel miserable in their bodies. I felt so far away from them, from everyone.

In the absence of a community of others, take the time to cultivate a safe space you can reliably turn to in moments of fear, of discomfort. We spend our entire lives with ourselves— this is why self-trust and self-love are crucial to our happiness and well-being. When our headspaces are true and safe, we can breathe easier. We can ask our bodies and our minds what we need to feel whole. We can listen with undivided attention. And we can act accordingly, to serve ourselves, to hold ourselves accountable.

At the time, I was more alone than I had ever been in my life. I felt misunderstood. I didn't believe I could change my life for the better. Without a purpose or connection, I lacked consistency in my healing. My mom compiled a list of professionals, and every day after school, there was a new appointment. I was stubborn and rude and made no effort to work with anyone who took the time to meet with me. It was not much of a surprise that nobody stuck. I don't mean to say that working with professionals isn't beneficial. I did ultimately get help, but it wasn't until I decided to become part of the solution that this happened. In the meantime, I saw dozens of therapists and psychiatrists. Their questions left me emotionally conflicted. I was sick of being sick, but I was terrified to step down from my position of power.

When asked to explain these conflicting thoughts, words failed me.

It went on and on and on like this.

The search for a dietician was similar. I was asked what foods I liked and struggled to form words. I had convinced myself I didn't like any foods because this made it easier to restrict my intake. The dietician tried, and I left our appointments clinging to a meal plan laced with foods I said I would eat but knew I wouldn't.

To be fair, I did push myself to face challenges in moments of confidence, but they were short-lived. I made weight for my next check-in, and the pediatrician was placated but not pleased. Nobody got their hopes up, not even me. I wish I had encouraged myself more and told myself something like this:

"Hey, that was difficult, and you're really tired. But that exhaustion just means you're working hard, and things will change for the better. It means something is happening, and isn't that what you want? Keep going."

Here's my theory about why recovery can be so difficult and why people in recovery sometimes stay stuck:

Even small moments of effort take a tremendous amount of mental energy.

It is emotionally taxing to challenge the rules set by an irrational internal voice.

Even small challenges can consume your mental focus for the entire day leading up to it, and then once you tackle that challenge, it becomes is all you think about afterward. How could this not take a toll on you?

I only truly got better when I accepted that recovery was going to be exhausting, all the time, always, taxing in every way, draining, painful, borderline unbearable—and then sticking with it anyway.

. . . .

I'm a visual person. I love seeing progress laid out in front of me. When I'm looking to hold myself accountable for making changes in my life now, I always map out a chart in my journal. There's an unmatched satisfaction that comes from filling in the date each day, followed by confirmation that yes, you know what? I did challenge myself today.

Here's a little chart to keep on hand. I strongly encourage you to replicate this and keep a long-form version of it somewhere safe. I keep mine in a notebook that sits on my desk. I've made charts like this when I'm looking to hold myself accountable for doing a nightly yoga flow before bed (helps me sleep better), stretching each morning (makes my body feel amazing), and drinking x amount of water throughout the day (hi, clear skin).

Knowing that I have a chart to report back to each day encourages me to stick with the commitment I've made to myself.

Today's date	How did I challenge myself today?	What is one thing I can do to continue this challenge?

Validating Yourself

I didn't understand recovery to be a fluid process. Instead, I saw it as these little isolated moments of resilience. Efforts I made occasionally. Efforts that felt overwhelmingly large.

Efforts that I put forth just to please my parents and to please my treatment team.

And frankly, just to be praised.

At that time, my commitment to recovery was rooted in people-pleasing and nothing more than that. I planned my recovery challenges around the schedules of others. If my mom wasn't home one afternoon to see me eating my snack before dinner, why should I even bother? So, I didn't. If I was left home alone and nobody was present to notice me not give in to the urge to exercise, why should I even resist?

I couldn't find strength within me in the absence of witnesses. What I could see externally was how others reacted to my actions. I could see when my doctors were pleased. I could see when my parents were disappointed. What I couldn't see were the small wins adding up to big shifts in my healing. That internal process was much slower than the instant feedback I received from my external world, and that was problematic in terms of my recovery.

Sometimes, we lose sight of our why. We may feel that we're going through the motions just to have someone tell us that we're doing something right. To validate our hard work. I think we all experience this need for validation to some degree, most notably in our interactions online. We seek likes, crave followers, strive for higher views. We want to be seen. We gauge how successful we are by someone else's attention.

I didn't understand that the true reason I should have been making these efforts to get better was to, well, get better. For me. To achieve genuine happiness, true health, deep freedom. These are internal measures. Since I couldn't see them in front of me, I never thought about them.

I spent a lot of time seeking external validation for my recovery efforts. I wanted to be praised for every little challenge I faced, every small fear I conquered. I was afraid that if someone wasn't around to notice the changes I was making, that they wouldn't "count." It was never enough for me to cheer myself on and hold myself accountable.

Consider this exercise more of a challenge. Today, make it a goal to do one thing that is healing for you that nobody else knows about. Something that may be hard, and may be scary, but something you're doing because you trust that this one small step is still a step, and it all adds up in the end. Do this for you you you you you.

Some examples of hard things to do that nobody sees:

- Opting for rest instead of movement if that's what your body is asking for
- Taking one day to eat meals that you're craving, instead of ones you planned ahead
- Posting a selfie when you feel happy and confident, without fear of judgment

On a day when you're itching for validation, turn back to this page. Remember what you accomplished when no one else was around. This day proves that you can do hard things without external validation. Keep going.

Chapter 5

Consequences

Strength Not in Numbers

From an outsider's perspective, it must have seemed that I loved the body I was in. I mean, I chose to look this way, right?

Not exactly.

I didn't *want* to look anorexic. I began my "diet" to change my body. But by the time my eating disorder had taken over my life, my body absolutely ached all of the time. Everything hurt. I felt unstable and weak. I despised being seen in public because I *knew* I was too small, too frail, too... sick. I didn't serve my disorder because I loved what it gave me. In fact, I *hated* what it took from me.

There came a point where I fell out of love with my illness.

My eating disorder had redefined the meaning of "strength" for me and forced me to prove that I was strong every single day. I believed that not eating meant I was strong. I believed that abusing my body with exercise meant

I was strong. I believed that cutting out x, y, and z meant I was strong.

This was the narrative my mind had fallen victim to.

I had chosen to follow the incorrect information I had found online. The sites I visited told me that eating less and moving more was equated with health. My disorder told me I was strong enough to be the healthiest person alive. All I had to do is push those two criteria to the absolute extreme.

I falsely believed that my body communicated messages about my worth to the world at large. That looking a certain way reflected my inner character. This couldn't be further from the truth. I want you to know that your value as a person and what you contribute to the world cannot be contained in your physical appearance. Your strength is proven to others through your actions, your commitment to overcoming hardship, and your dedication to true health and happiness.

I was tired and miserable one morning when my mother knocked on my bedroom door.

"It's Mom; open up."

She peeked into my room and told me I was squeezed in for a weigh-in before school. On my way out of the room, I caught a glimpse of my reflection and wished it would disappear. My face was draped in skin so pale that, for a moment, I thought I could see through myself completely.

Regardless of how committed I was to what I believed at the time was progress, I still hated the way I looked. Your pursuit of health and happiness shouldn't leave you self-loathing. Recognizing this discomfort is crucial to turning your relationship with your body back around. Reevaluate the choices you've become so dedicated to. Are they serving you? Do you feel guilty for not following a specific diet? Do you only feel accomplished when others validate you through compliments or likes online? Your strength is yours to define. It's a concept much bigger than the shape of your body, how toned it is, how small. How strong was I, really, if I couldn't even handle looking at my reflection?

When I look back at that time, I wonder if I would have been able to heal more quickly if I had the supportive community I have now. If I had a group of people who understood my feelings and could have shown me ways to overcome the troubles I faced, to prove that there was a way out and they had found it—that might have made all the difference. To see firsthand that my present was someone else's past, to understand that there was a life to be hand beyond the rules and obsessions I had fallen into.

But back then, the car was running when I stepped outside, and both of my parents were inside. A few minutes into the ride, I realized something was off.

"Mom? Mom, didn't you tell Dad we have an appointment? I'm going to be late for school."

Slowly she turned around to face me from the passenger seat.

She just looked at me.

My blood ran cold when we pulled into a parking lot, and I began kicking, screaming, and crying.

The next thing I knew, my dad was pulling me out of the backseat by my waist as I lay face down, trying to grip something, anything, to keep me in the car.

Eventually, I lost steam and was thrown over my dad's shoulder, folded over at my middle and dangling on both ends.

That was how I entered the hospital. Talk about strength.

Once I was admitted, I was angry. At the time, I believed that anger and strength were entwined and that my anger made me strong. I now know that I was wrong.

When I was sick, I was irrational, selfish, and defensive. I couldn't see offers of help for what they were (*extensions of love and support*); instead, I saw them as threats to my strength and power.

Once I was able to think clearly again, I understood that the feelings of anger I held toward my parents on that day weren't justified. With that understanding, I made my way toward forgiveness and acceptance. What a breath of fresh air it was to feel the last bits of deep anger slip off my being like rain. It was cleansing.

If you are anything like me, you may find yourself dismissive of other people's sides of the story. I often fixate on myself and the pain I face due to their actions, which causes me to overlook their *"why."* I sometimes forget to ask what led them to the decision that caused me anger in the first place. This insight has played an instrumental role in my ability to release feelings of anger.

If possible, keep in mind that when it comes to others' intervention in your life (when some sort of disorder is involved), their intentions are likely pure. They simply want to see the person they care about thrive and be well. From the outside, they can see that person is hurting but this may be difficult to recognize for people invested in the disordered life they've built.

When someone in your life tries to intervene, you may feel threatened. You may direct feelings of anger toward them for trying to get you help, asking if you're okay/checking in, calling you out on toxic behaviors. It's easy to turn to anger because you may feel that this person is trying to take something away from you when really, they're trying to give you something back: Your health. Your well-being. Your peace of mind.

It may help to view the situation from their perspective to see yourself as they see you.

See if you can answer these questions: (Try to be as objective as you possibly can.)

What did this person say/do that hurt you?

_____

_____

_____

_____

_____

_____

_____

_____

_____

What do they have to gain from this action?

_____

_____

_____

_____

What do you have to gain from this action?

_____

_____

_____

_____

_____

If the roles were reversed, would you do the same for them?

_____

_____

_____

_____

_____

Creating Your Own Comfort

At the hospital, a large, overstuffed binder sat on the bedside table. I flipped through it before dinner. The gist of the program was as follows: I was going to be assigned a nutritionist, a therapist, and a psychiatrist. There were several caloric plans that I would move through during my stay. The nutritionist's job was to safely increase my intake. We would work together to plan out my meals and snacks for the week based on a value system of starches, fats, proteins, etc. I would meet with my therapist once a day and could call on them more as needed. The doctor only needed to see me weekly to oversee my weight-gain process.

In between all these appointments, I passed the days in group therapy sessions, in "school," and meals.

There were "levels" that indicated how well-behaved and compliant I was as a patient. Completing meals, participating in group sessions, socializing with the other patients, making progress in therapy, and most importantly, gaining weight, granted me a positive review so I would be rewarded by going up a "level." Eventually, when my level was high enough, I was granted a "weekend pass," which allowed me to leave the hospital for a day trip on the weekends.

But that first day, my heart was heavy, and I was tired from battling a tornado of anxiety. I felt physically sick, overwhelmed with rules, unfamiliar faces, and the faint, constant hum of overhead hospital lights over my bed.

I was lonely. I had been lonely for quite some time. Isolating myself and prioritizing food, exercise, and body image over relationships and memories had left me emotionally disconnected from everyone else.

You don't need to be sitting alone in the hospital to identify with this feeling. The good news is, it's never too late to begin closing the emotional gap between yourself and those you love. The first step to reducing the distance between you and others is to come back to yourself. Again, this idea of being your own support system is essential. If we are out of touch with ourselves, we can't expect to truly be in touch with those around us. You need to show yourself grace and respect for where you are in your present moment and look forward to the relationship growth you will find in the future. This is self-love at its core. It's acceptance, and with that will come connection. Loneliness only hinders your ability to grow. Connection and community are key factors in healing. Give these to yourself first, and you will find them out in the world shortly after.

A bell rang down the hall. Time for dinner.

Everyone, no matter what their life circumstances, will at some point find themselves facing difficult, maybe even frightening, situations on their own. When I was alone in this hospital facing one of my biggest fears, I wished I had known how to give myself comfort and strength. This exercise is a way for you to build up your internal strength for the times when you may need it. The community I have built through social media has also given me support to help me get through the hard times.

Here are the tools. Remember to sharpen them each day.

To practice, I ask myself what I would say to support someone I care about if they were in a frightening situation. What would I say to comfort them? Write these "you are" statements to someone you care about.

You are_____.

You are_____.

You are_____.

Then I go back to these statements and swap "you are" for "I am."

I am _____.

I am _____.

I am _____.

Read these back to yourself each day. They will become deeply ingrained, and maybe, just maybe, you'll begin to hold them as truths. When you find yourself alone and afraid, call on them. *Love yourself the way you love those around you.*

Chapter 6

Growth

Healing Starts from Within

If, at the time, I had the support community I have cultivated through social media, I would have understood that I wasn't alone. Knowing that others had similar experiences would have given me strength. But I didn't have that community yet, and I felt entirely isolated.

My first in-patient dinner was like jumping into a pool and forgetting how to swim.

A nurse sat in the corner of the dining room with a clipboard and a stopwatch. Every meal was monitored and timed. I followed the other patients through the door, and she rose from her chair to introduce me as the "newest group member."

I smiled weakly and nodded. Nobody said a word.

Great.

A food cart was wheeled in.

We had forty-five minutes to finish. Nobody spoke; it was quiet, save for the occasional crunch and chew or slurp of juice. My grilled cheese sat wrapped in a square of tinfoil. A helpless cry from a deeply neglected corner of my mind shrieked, "Just do it! Eat it!"

So, I did.

One bite. Then two. A few more, and the first half was gone. Twenty minutes went by, and I hadn't touched the other half. To my genuine surprise, everyone was close to finishing their meal.

If they can do it, I can too, I thought. So I did. I finished.

It's amazing that this micro-community, just a small room filled with a handful of people, was able to spark a sense of true strength within me. A shared understanding that we had all walked similar paths that led us to this moment was comforting. For the first time, I was surrounded by people who knew the weight of the pain I had felt. Pain I had truly believed I was alone in bearing.

A timer blared from the corner of the room. One by one, we were each asked if we had finished our meal. Our answers were charted. When my name was called, I released a breath that I must had been holding since the beginning of roll call. "Complete" meant I had finished; I had eaten, I had given in. "Incomplete" meant I had resisted. In my disordered mind, it meant I was strong.

I said the word that made me feel both triumphant and like a failure: "Complete."

My final task of the day was to sleep, and even though I was exhausted, and my eyelids kept drooping, my mind was in overdrive. I tossed and turned, and with each flip, I swore

I could feel the grilled cheese tumbling around, taunting me. Mental gymnastics lulled me into slumber.

The next day was a long one. I was able to get through breakfast with more ease than dinner. I passed the time in between meals meeting with my treatment team.

"The most important thing, of course, is reaching your goal weight," the doctor emphasized to the room.

Would I be healed then? What exactly did it mean to be healed?

Instead of asking, I remained quiet and nodded. In this program, gaining weight was the sole sign of progress. It was the only key back into the real world.

I was expected to trust these people to heal me, even though I didn't understand how they would do it.

Physical manifestations of healing, like reaching a goal weight and facing fear foods, didn't feel sufficient. That's because true healing is an internal shift. It takes place not where you can see it but where you can feel it. It is the total of small steps, little actions, and mindset changes that you stick to, day in and day out. Healing happens when you choose your individual, unique health and happiness over and over again, and cancel external noise and pressure that tells you to do differently.

I encourage you to learn everything you can about what is happening with your body and mind. Information is strength, and making sure you are getting accurate information is key.

I was told I was anorexic. My doctors focused on physical issues: my weight loss, my shortness of breath, my slow heart, and so on. I didn't know that eating disorders are rooted in thoughts and fears. I was told I needed to "recover." I was told this meant reversing the physical and internal bodily damage I had caused until that point.

I was there to treat the physical ailments, not the mental ones, but in hindsight, the mental ones were dictating the physical ones.

I knew that I felt nervous in my own company. I knew that my mind-space was a dark place.

I didn't know that healing began from mending *those* wounds: the ones I couldn't see.

. . . .

I didn't know anything about the disorder I was dying from. Since then, I have found the same is true for others with varying types of disorders.

I didn't know how to express how poor my mental health was, and nobody asked. I wrote a lot during this time in treatment. We were given composition notebooks to keep track of our thoughts if we wanted. I used mine every single night. I spilled words onto the page with vigor, eager to get the toxic thoughts and paranoia out of my mind by way of my fingertips.

Most of my writing was focused on food and my body, and all of it was negative. This felt like the norm for me, so at the time, I didn't understand how unhealthy it was. But if I had shown someone even one day's worth of what I had written—the thoughts that felt safe only on paper—I do believe more attention would have been given to my mental state.

Sometimes it's easier to write what is too difficult to say. Here's space for you to express your true thoughts and feelings.

Today's date	Thought/feeling I had

Finding Your Voice

Having a consistent therapist felt foreign. We met daily in my room.

Talking was difficult, regardless of how much I enjoyed my therapist's company. Questions about my favorite subject in school were juxtaposed with more serious questions. "What thoughts came to mind when you sat down for lunch earlier? Were you scared? What behaviors did you want to use?"

Being asked to explain my fears out loud required me to turn anxieties into words, and when the words made no sense together, I heard how irrational my thoughts were. Saying things like, "I am scared to eat a bagel because it's going to make me fat," was humiliating and absurd.

This was the first time I understood what the disorder was doing to my mind. But my disorder was louder than logic, at least then. My therapist was more focused on restoring my weight than understanding what was going on in my mind, so we didn't address how delusional my beliefs were. Instead, we focused on breathwork, making pros and cons lists about arbitrary things, and developing mechanisms to ensure I could finish each meal. Between sessions, I completed assignments to keep my mind busy, which helped me breathe a little easier.

I watched patients came and go; sometimes, they lasted only a few days.

All I could think about was going home. My skin felt tight. My body felt distant and was growing larger. I wanted it to stop.

By the time Thanksgiving rolled around, I had received a day pass to join my family for the holiday.

The day zoomed by. My relatives knew where I had been. It felt like everyone was walking on glass when they approached me, hugged me lightly, and pulled away quickly.

The holiday season can be difficult for anyone struggling with emotional disorders, disordered eating, or body issues. More often than not, the holidays are a prime time for family and friends to come together and socialize, with the high likelihood of various triggers sneaking into the conversational mix. The person saying them is likely *unaware* that they are causing you harm or discomfort. These comments are coming from a place of heavy media influence.

At the dinner table, my relatives spoke of new diets they had been on in anticipation of the big holiday meal. Someone reached for seconds even though they let us know that they *really shouldn't*. A cousin made plans with another cousin to hit the gym the next day to *burn off* the food they ate. My mom fixed a plate for me, and I panicked. My brain hurt as it ping-ponged between all these triggering comments. How did this conversation feel so *normal* for everyone else? It no longer felt normal to me.

You can't control every conversation you'll be forced to hear. If you're easily triggered, remember your power. If a relative is speaking about bodies, food, weight, exercise, mental health, or *whatever* it is that puts you on edge, remember your voice.

Speak up. If you find the conversation triggering, remove yourself from it. Assert yourself. Something as simple as, "I'd prefer to speak about other things, if you don't mind," can go a long way. It forces the other person to reflect on what is being said. It also allows you to protect yourself.

One way to take care of yourself is to be prepared to redirect the conversation. If you have a social gathering coming up, set a few minutes aside the day before or the morning of the event to map out potential comments and answers.

Here are some examples:

> *If they say: "I've been putting on so much weight, I need to work out harder/longer."*
>
> *You can say: "As long as you're living a life that's healthy and happy for you, that's all that matters."*

> *If they say: "You look good/fit/thin/etc."*
>
> *You can say: "I'm focusing more on how I feel inside, but I appreciate your kindness."*

> *If they say: "I hate the way my body looks."*
>
> *You can say: "Call to mind all of the wonderful things your body allows you to do each day and hold this to a higher degree of importance than what it looks like."*

Try some of these out on your own and arm yourself with potential responses as a guide for when an uncomfortable moment presents itself. Sometimes a trigger will feel strong, but remember that you have the power—and a plan—to face them.

Chapter 7

Stuck

Fall Down Nine, Get Up Ten

After what seemed like forever, I was allowed to leave the hospital and return home as an outpatient.

At the exit from the hospital, I paused. Outside the sliding glass doors, the sun was setting. It was almost five o'clock, and the sky felt heavy with opaque silhouettes of trees glued against an amber sky.

Now that I was home and my every move wasn't monitored, all the old rules my disorder created resurfaced. I fell back into old behaviors.

And so, the vicious cycle began again. Bouncing from one new therapist to the next, no stable dietician, same old, same old. I was back to weekly check-ups with the pediatrician. I tormented my parents, forced them to question where they went wrong. *How did we let this happen?* It was not their fault.

When I returned to school, it was the last week before winter break. After two months at home, the weight was already gone. My behaviors were strong, and my body was weak. I was stuck. I spent almost all of my time in my room. I felt safe in isolation, free to fall back into old ways. I didn't know how to deal with the discomforts of my healing, my body changing, my old world turning into a new one. I didn't know how to let go and be okay all on my own. My inability to cope with this process stemmed from my lack of a community.

When challenging toxic thoughts became too hard, I ran from them. I didn't allow myself to lean on others or even myself because this meant I would have to face the truth—that I had work to do and that this work was hard.

It wouldn't have felt so hard if I had realized the problems I faced were not mine alone. That other people felt these struggles too. The world is large, and there are people out there who know the struggles you face. You must be willing to find them. Body image, emotional disabilities, and related issues are more common than you may believe. They simply aren't talked about as often or openly as they should be—as much as they need to be.

The only way to become comfortable talking about uncomfortable things is to, well, get uncomfortable. Be willing to start difficult conversations with the people in your life. You'll be surprised to find that even if two people haven't gone through the same situation, they can find bits and pieces of each other's stories that they identify with and relate to. This is comforting.

You have work to do, but you don't have to do it alone.

For this exercise, approach someone in your life who you trust and respect. Maybe that's a parent, sibling, friend, or coworker. Begin by telling them you have been struggling, and then talk to them about some of the roadblocks that have prevented you from finding healing. You can be vague—sharing details can be difficult in the beginning.

Here are some examples:

- "I'm having a hard time feeling confident in my body. Have you ever felt something like this?"
- "Sometimes scrolling online makes me feel anxious. Do you ever feel this way?"

Community is founded on connection and common understanding. When you open up these conversations with other people, you can begin to build this sense of community. You will be less inclined to isolate yourself and bear your burdens alone if you're aware that there are other people out there who get it. Community is a resource. Lean on it.

I Think, Therefore I Am

In late February, I was admitted to the hospital again.
I had a lot more work to do this time around. There was
more weight to put on, sure, but after my last stay, there were
plenty of mental hurdles to navigate as well.

Even though the experience wasn't new, it still hurt
all the same. A certain pain came with having to live in a
hospital while the outside world flowed on, day in and day
out, functioning perfectly fine without me. I felt small and
pointless. As if I contributed nothing at all.

While my last stay was marked by resistance and an empty
mind, my second round had me thinking. I visualized myself
with powerful legs that supported a heart filled with peace
and skin rich with life. I visualized myself pulsing with light. I
could see the possibility of high color in my cheeks and a laugh
always on the tip of my tongue. But there was work to be done
to get to the place I could see in my mind's eye. From a dim
corner room in the eating disorders unit, I began the work,
slowly piecing together the girl I longed to be.

Mental healing came in waves. Group therapy sessions
were unpredictable, some pointless and others moving. The
groups my therapist led were my favorite.

One week, we were given a basket of old magazines, safety
scissors, glue sticks, and construction paper. Our task was to
create a recovery vision board. The project was empowering.
Dreams big and small found homes on my board, and each
swipe of the glue stick cranked my healthy voice a notch
louder. I found a part of me that *wanted* to heal.

I assumed the role of stellar patient. I participated in
groups and made conversation with the other patients. Most

importantly, I stopped begging to go home. I was doing everything I could to make this stay different from my first. The goal was to get out and *stay* out.

Everything else was the same. Each day I sat in a room with tiled floors and tiled walls with hard plastic chairs arranged in a circle. Each day I sat through group therapy sessions that were often repetitive and sometimes ineffective.

Although I wanted to be better, I sometimes found myself slipping into old habits of self-sabotage. When I met with my therapist, I provided all the right answers. Everything she wanted to hear, responses that painted a picture of strength. Although I wanted to stay out and be healthy, I still couldn't quite entirely buy into what therapy was offering me.

All of my perfect answers allowed me to return to school. I finished out the year exempt from my finals and avoiding my friends. I endured a long heartfelt check-in after class from one of my favorite teachers, who was thrilled to have me back and see me "doing well." My heart hit the floor. This new body didn't mean I was better. It made me anxious. I was always on edge, and I wanted to jump out of my skin.

Self-love is a lifelong process. You will be many, many selves throughout your lifetime. As you grow older and change and move into new seasons of your life, you may have to actively work on loving a new version of yourself each time. It may be difficult to leave old versions of yourself behind because they were familiar, especially past bodies. Focus your self-love efforts on appreciating what this new body allows you to achieve, the life it allows you to live, how full that is, how empowering. How your legs are strong and able to hold you up each day. How your stomach holds deep belly laughs that you share with your closest friends. How your arms are your means of giving and receiving hugs.

Perspective shapes our world. How we see our world directly influences how happy we are. I could have seen my weight-restored body in two radically different ways: The first one from a place of gratitude for my improving health. The second from a place of despair. *What have I lost by "giving in"?*

When I was living in the hospital, my perspective through which I viewed my world was of working toward being a healthy weight. I had internalized images of peace and happiness in my future. But once back home, without the confines of the therapeutic structure of the hospital program, I relapsed again. I had lost a support system that would have allowed me to ground that perception.

· ·

You are your own worst critic. Your perspective when addressing yourself may be hard to trust. Consulting friends and family for their perspectives on different aspects of you as a person can help you step away from yourself and give you a healthy dose of reality.

Think of something about yourself that may make you uncomfortable. Maybe this is your height. Now think about how you would address yourself regarding this discomfort. It might be something negative, along the lines of telling yourself you can't wear heels because you would be too tall.

Next, think of this same issue from the perspective of another person. What would a friend tell you about your height? They might encourage you to appreciate how uniquely it allows you to view the world. Or note that you can easily reach things you need in the kitchen without using a step stool. Talk about a shift in perspective.

The truth is, nobody thinks about you as much as you do. Internalizing this truth can feel like release. Fill out the chart below. View yourself through the eyes of a loving friend.

Discomfort	What I would say	What a friend would say

Chapter 8

Rewiring

Breaking Up with Control

Those around me saw a weight-restored girl and used this visual to gauge my progress. They perceived healing when they should have been asking about the state of my emotions instead. The will to get better was there. Some part of me, small and microscopic, knew there was more for me in this life than an untimely death. But despite knowing it, I couldn't quite find a way to live into it.

The fears my eating disorder had planted in my mind were nourished by starvation, and the influx of self-care destroyed them slowly, from the top down, working toward the root, until I could finally start to see past them. The most prominent of these fears came in the form of worrying that I was losing control.

One day spent in recovery was a pure loss of control. I felt like a bystander as I watched my body change. I knew I wanted to escape my sick body, but it was so hard.

I tried to control every teeny situation in my life and somehow expected to live at peace. Peace comes when you are accepting of your role in the universe. Not everything is yours to control. You can't control the subconscious instinct to compare yourself with the bodies you see online. But you can control how you react to it and how you let these feelings play a role in your next actions. As a perfectionist, I was so fixated on perfecting my body; nothing else occupied my thoughts. I was addicted to measuring myself. I felt accomplished because I had tangible means of gauging progress—meals skipped and made smaller, workouts added and made longer. Instead of spending time thinking about my body and every factor contributing to its make-up, I should have started a hobby or volunteered, anything that would have given me some temporary release.

Losing weight and committing to toxic habits was easier than restoring my health because diet culture had taught me that the first two feats were praised. Standing by both made me feel like I was doing something right, which made the discomfort seem worthwhile. Restoring my health was much, much harder. This is because I never saw or even heard of anyone firsthand rebelling against diet culture in the way I was supposed to be doing. I had to be my own example. And this pressure was heavy.

I felt hopelessly stuck. I was angry with myself for not being better and for wasting so much time. At this point, I longed for health, but I understood the journey to be grueling: emotionally, physically, and mentally. I let this hold me back and hated myself for it. I truly realized how dangerous my disorder was. The lengths I was willing to go to protect it were humiliating and extreme.

And yet, I couldn't stop.

. . . .

Many people who struggle with disordered relationships with themselves tend to be Type A or perfectionists in nature. We look for the things we can control. We find an extreme degree of safety and comfort that comes from always knowing what to expect.

And as an extension, we feel an extreme degree of discomfort when the future is unknown.

This exercise requires some off-the-page effort.

For this exercise, surrender control for just one day. Go into a (safe) experience that challenges you. It's okay to be scared. It's okay to fail. It's even okay to just exist out of your comfort zone. The point is that you try something that you can't control.

Once you're done, write down what you felt. There are no wrong answers.

*Today I*_____

_____.

*This made me feel*_____.

. . . .

Stigma Is Judgment in Disguise

As months went by, my mood swings and sulking nature were amplified. My mom informed me she made an appointment with a doctor to discuss my "depressive symptoms." Initially, I was angry and defensive. But after a beat, I realized I was also relieved she had said the words I couldn't form myself.

A week later, my mom and I walked into a family medical practice. For once, I decided to give an honest response rather than what I thought I was supposed to say when the doctor began to ask me questions. I was burnt out from masking the truth. I was done standing in my own way.

Dr. L asked about my friends, and I let him know I had none. He asked about my hobbies, and I let him know I had none. He asked about my favorite foods, and I let him know, again, that I had none.

He asked if I ever felt sad for no reason. If I could go from happy to sad in a matter of minutes. If I felt unmotivated, and if so, about what. Did I lash out at my parents and then feel upset afterward? Regretful?

He believed I was suffering from significant depression and general anxiety. We would start with a small dose of an antidepressant/anti-anxiety medication and work our way up every few weeks. The words were terrifying, but I trusted him to help me.

I saw my situation like this: I was standing at rock bottom and was holding a shovel, threatening to dig deeper. And then, I saw—at last—the option to trade in the shovel for other tools, like a little orange bottle filled with little white tablets that would help me climb up instead of down. I didn't have to keep breaking ground, slipping deeper and deeper into crevices below. I was hopeful but still deathly afraid. I struggled to accept that I needed medication to function.

But I asked myself, if not now, then when? How much time was left on my side?

I had been resisting full commitment to reclaiming my health and wellness due to self-judgment. Without realizing it, you too may be judging yourself based on stigmas you've come to internalize. Recovering from a damaged body image is a process that cannot unfold in the presence of judgment. For so long, I knew I needed help but feared pursuing many options because I believed they would reflect poorly on my character. There is no one way to recover. Your recovery will reflect your individual needs and align with your definition of health. Try and think of this as exciting. Your self-love journey is all your own. When you view it through this lens of individuality, you may no longer feel inclined to judge and compare the process.

There can be a stigma surrounding medications to manage mental illness or emotional disabilities, which discourages some people from exploring this option.

Though I can only speak from my experience, which is a mild case compared to more severe disorders and conditions, I whole-heartedly believe that medicating helped stabilize me enough to begin truly healing. To say that brain chemistry is complex is an understatement, but the medical treatments available to people suffering from mental or emotional disorders continue to expand as research into the field continues.

Is it time for you to challenge this belief? Are you guilty of swearing off medication? Why is that? Have you bought into a societal stigma about this treatment option? Medication may or may not be the best course of action for you, but the important thing is to consider all avenues for seeking help. Sometimes you may need something small and temporary to set a foundation for something big and long-lasting.

Our mental health can be an uncomfortable topic to talk about due to widespread stigmas. Imagine you want to start a conversation about your mental health with another person, maybe a parent, teacher, or a boss. Would this trigger a sense of anxiety or discomfort? What stigmas can you think of that might make this feat challenging? Write these down.

_____

_____

_____

_____

Now read these back. Are the above beliefs true? Are they worth keeping silent for and not seeking the help you need? Remember that by letting fear of judgment control you, you're only hurting yourself. Healing begins with acceptance, with the willingness to do what's right even when it feels hard.

Self-Love Begins with Forgiveness

After a few weeks, I concluded that either the pills were working, or a placebo effect was in full swing. Either way, I felt lighter. The little things that usually sent me spiraling were seemed more manageable. Not easy, but manageable.

One day, while I was still lingering in a soft safe space of quasi-recovery, I was out in the backyard when I heard flip-flopped footsteps. Small and quick. It was my little sister.

She circled to the front of my chair and sat on the edge near my feet. In her hands, she held a bowl of beautiful red grapes.

For a few minutes, we sat in silence. Then my sister popped a grape in her mouth, and I heard the skin burst between her teeth. It rattled between my ears. She turned to me and offered one. One single grape.

Despite how calm and collected I had been feeling on my medication, anxiety welled up from every deep corner, swirled to my core, and turned to dead weight.

I lost control and yanked the bowl out of her hands and threw the grapes. My sister had run into the house. The grapes were gone. My disorder was satisfied with our performance. Hunger pangs ripped across my abdomen. I felt regret. I was angry. I was frustrated. And then I realized what I had done.

I knew I was better than that.

I stood up and headed inside to the fridge. I pulled out more grapes, which I washed and dumped in a bowl. My mom sat on a chair at the table, my sister crying in her lap, and the two of them quietly watched as the scene unfolded.

Then I placed a grape in my mouth. And then another and another. When I was finished with the bowl, I threw my arms around the two of them, and we cried together until we didn't need to anymore. Finally, it was all out.

What a pleasure it was to cry in the arms of others. I wanted more of this. I wanted more tears because they reminded me that I was alive, and I wanted more of that too.

This was the first true moment I felt forgiveness in my self-love journey. I felt forgiveness toward those I perceived as having hurt me and forgiveness toward myself and my body.

I felt triggered when I heard the crunch of the grape, and in the absence of healthy coping mechanisms, I lashed out. I let anger fuel me, but then I saw how I was behaving. For the first time, I saw how my actions were affecting my family.

The need for forgiveness from them entered the equation. I saw the pain in my sister's eyes. I realized how innocent her efforts were to simply connect to me and to help me help myself. When I came down from the panic, it was the need for forgiveness that brought me to the fridge and lifted each grape to my mouth. It was an effort to remedy my previous actions. It was my way of apologizing to my sister, my mother, and even myself. Forgiveness is a powerful tool in restoring self-love and healthy body image.

When you accept that you have made unhealthy choices in the past, you can hold yourself accountable and work hard to make healthier decisions moving forward. You can come to a place of peace with who you were and, therefore, who you will become. You can grow. You can be more than your past. You can recreate yourself over and over and over again.

I knew I had to forgive myself—and you should forgive yourself, too. I had to forgive my body for the pain it caused me and others. I had to own who I had been for so long to become someone better moving forward. On this journey, I learned how forgiveness could also help us cope, heal, and grow.

Forgiveness heals.

For years, I held this memory close to my heart, and it pierced me. My mind sometimes raced when I thought about how frightened my sister must have been and about how irrational and absurd I had behaved. Feelings of embarrassment and regret and shame swirled within me.

I held onto those feelings and never mentioned them to my sister because I was ashamed of who I was at that moment. I had so many ways to say I was sorry, but I needed to release them.

Think of a time when you hurt someone you loved to protect your disordered relationship with yourself. In that moment, what did you take from that person?

Reflect deeply and selflessly.

Now—how would you apologize to them? What would you say? How many ways can you release this deep-seated regret? How many words, how many gestures?

Write this down. The weight of those negative feelings is reduced when they find a new home on the page.

_____

_____

_____

_____

_____

_____

_____

_____

_____

_____

_____

_____

Take it one step further and share your words with the person you have hurt, if possible. It can feel daunting to pour your heart out and then trust someone else to hold these words in their hands. But think about it this way: if you felt such a deep release from reading them, you owe the other person involved the chance to experience this too. Whether they are receptive or not is not up to you. All you can do is say you are sorry and mean it. Let that be enough.

Chapter 9

Self-Care

You Are Whole

Trust in your healing process is key when developing new habits. Trusting yourself can feel scary; letting go of the rules and beliefs that have grown familiar might make you feel that you are in unknown territory. And to a certain extent, you are, but that is okay. It gives you time to discover the wonderful things you didn't even know about yourself. Take the time to nurture yourself and, by extension, find a nurturing community.

The grape war with my sister triggered an epiphany that saved my life and brought me back to my family. I stopped being at odds with them and instead allowed them to care for me. Every morning from that day on, I woke up and stubbornly renewed the dreaded commitment I made to healing my relationship with food, my body, and myself.

I had known for years that my disorder was not mine alone. The time I spent sick was time my family spent suffering too. How had I not noticed how anxious my sisters felt around me as if I could break in half at any moment? How had I not noticed the fear in my parents' eyes when I walked into a room? I never wanted to see the people I love most in pain, and yet I had done exactly that. The realization didn't sit well with me. They deserved better, and so did I.

My full recovery began with weight restoration, which was difficult but even more difficult in the height of summer because that time of year brings so much focus on weight loss and bikini bodies. When growing smaller was praised, I was pursuing the complete opposite. I viewed myself as an outcast, which was difficult and wildly uncomfortable.

I worried that I would be on the outskirts for the rest of my life, always a special case, an exception, and wrong. Yet, as I consistently nourished my body, my mind reaped endless benefits. I was able to think more clearly and more rationally.

The first few weeks of weight gain were laced with frustration. I wanted to trust my body to do the right thing.

I had never asked myself that before.

Do I trust my body?

I was trying.

Positive self-talk was my disorder's kryptonite. It came in many forms. Verbally and in thought, but mostly in writing. I began keeping a daily journal, using the Notes app on my iPhone. I wrote daily entries. Some were boring; I recounted what I ate that day and if it rained. Others were heavily charged, written during a panic attack.

Some sentences ran on for pages. My journal was my coping mechanism. Between venting out loud to my parents and through written words on my iPhone screen, I moved closer to a state of peace, stability, and acceptance. I was finally giving my healthy inner voice a time to shine. I was finally listening. And in listening, I began to establish trust with my body. I would let myself write without judgment of my words. Thoughts, needs, desires, and fears spilled on the page before me, and for the first time, I didn't silence or suppress them. Instead, I allowed them to be real and accepted them as valid. Then I gave my body what it was asking for, which was an appropriate amount of nourishment. I could feel myself begin to thrive.

I want you to take this time to read back the words you've written so far in the prompts in this book. Read them slowly. Sit with them. What resonates with you? Do you notice patterns in what you have written? Do you feel new emotions reading old ones?

Read your past work and answer this—in a few words, a sentence, a paragraph, a novel, however you may choose.

Who are you?

_____

_____

_____

_____

_____

Find yourself in your words.

What do you love about your body? What can you give it to show your appreciation and gratitude for it?

_____

_____

_____

_____

_____

_____

_____

_____

_____

We may not have control over many things in our lives, but we possess the power to define and honor ourselves. How others choose to define us is reflective of their character, not ours. When we can finally accept this, we can tap into our truest person. All it takes is a bit of digging, some listening, and a willingness to try, to learn.

Cultivating Community

Recovery wasn't an end destination for me. It was and is a process, and it will be lifelong.

Weight restoration was riddled with changes that left me confused and afraid. Nobody prepared me for what to expect. Some days I wondered if this was all backfiring. Even eating small amounts made my body feel too full, and that feeling was uncomfortable for me both physically and emotionally.

But then I asked myself, *so what should I do about it?*

I realized I had two options. I could have stopped my recovery in hopes that the symptoms would go away. But then I'd be sick again and back at square one. Or I could keep working on getting healthier, on trusting that the uncomfortable feelings would pass, and having enough faith in the higher power that I believed looked over me. I reminded myself that all discomfort was truly temporary.

I chose the second option, and it was hard; it was hell, and I wanted to run away from it pretty much every day, but something kept me hanging on. As time passed and recovery settled deeper into my bones, life grew wider, and it slowly became mine to keep and to love.

The weight came on, and I watched myself transform. I began to see the beauty of healing, health, self-care, and self-love. I began to respect the importance of physical and emotional nourishment.

My skin began to flush with color. The weight was redistributed across my frame. Energy began to flood my tank, and I no longer grew exhausted after small efforts. Slowly I was revitalized.

It was enough to keep me going and to continue the work. I cultivated a lust for life. I saw it in my eyes, and I never wanted to lose it again.

The summer I embarked on my recovery came to an end, and I began my senior year of high school.

On the morning of my last first day, I was on my way out the door with a packed lunch I planned to eat. On that day, I didn't stuff a heavy sweater in my backpack to keep me warm because, for the first time in years, I was able to withstand an air-conditioned classroom just like the rest of my peers.

I thought back to the girl I had been the year before: the girl who passed the school day crying in the bathroom. The girl who went days without saying a single word out loud, speaking to nobody but the voice in her head.

I had become someone new. I had passions and gratitude.

Somewhere along this whole journey, I fell in love with food. I finally began to see it as sustenance. It saved my life. As I ate more, I gained much more beyond weight. My brain could think without feeling foggy. My heart could love openly.

It turned out I adored food and had all along. I had just been suppressing it. Growing up in a large Italian family, I was nothing if not a foodie. My parents taught me from a young age that eating is an act of nurture, care, dedication, and commitment. Food is an honoring of culture and tradition, a way to celebrate those who have passed and those here now. Eating consistently again revitalized this love for food.

The years I spent demonizing food were ones I spent out of touch with my loved ones. Once I began to mend this disordered relationship with nourishment, I was able to sit at the dinner table in the company of others, with a clear head and a focus on the present moment. One of my favorite things about food is that it provides a vehicle to show love to both ourselves and others. Every person needs food, in some form, to stay alive. We can all bond through our shared need for nourishment. When your relationship with food is strong and stable, it makes every other relationship in your life that much easier: with body image, mindfulness, loved ones, and most importantly, yourself.

I was reminded of all of this as I sat in the driver's seat on that warm September morning, waiting for my sister to come outside so I could drive us to school. How far I had come and how far I had yet to go.

I couldn't wait to meet the person I would become tomorrow, the next day, and the next.

· ·

"Today, you could be standing next to someone who is trying their very best not to fall apart. So, whatever you do today, do it with kindness in your heart."

I recently saw that saying on a sign outside a coffee shop. It's stuck with me ever since. You never, ever know who needs to hear a word of encouragement to keep trekking on. You must be a safe space for yourself so you can be a safe space for others. You must be your own support system so you can positively play a role in someone else's network as well. When you mend your relationships with food and body image, you become safe and trust yourself. You can, then, extend your support and kindness to everyone you cross paths with.

Issues related to food and body image are rooted internally, in a place beyond what can be seen on the surface. You can't see at first glance who is lacking a community. Assume that someone can always benefit from connection and, if possible, provide that for others.

This exercise is more of a daily practice than a single writing prompt.

Take time each day to help someone else hold themselves up by doing something as simple as sending a kind text or smiling from across the room. Kindness can bring someone one step closer to saving themselves.

We grow together.

Be a part of the community that saves someone and that saves yourself.

Part II:

After Social Media

Chapter 10

Getting Started

It feels nearly impossible to approach the topic of social media without negative concepts like "comparison traps" and "highlight reels" looming overhead. These feel like dark threats to our well-being.

When the idea to start dieting initially crossed my mind, the internet transformed into my Bible, a canon I followed blindly into toxic darkness. Long nights were spent hunched over my family's desktop, clicking and clicking and clicking, one hyperlink to the next.

Those online spaces were black holes. I fell in, and I fell fast. I didn't know better. I was so desperate for guidance that I took anyone's word without questioning the accuracy or even the intention behind it. I was easily influenced. I didn't know myself very well because, for so long, I silenced my body and my heart when they both desperately tried to communicate with me. The content I consumed there was my first taste of toxic habits.

There's no denying it—social media is notorious for causing consumers to feel inadequate. How often have you heard about people experiencing depressive symptoms as a direct result of social media? Far too many. How many of us can identify with an experience along those lines? Far, *far* too many.

But what happens when users capitalize on the benefits of social media and online communities, such as its ability to connect us with like-minded individuals all around the world, who we otherwise would have had no idea even existed? What happens when users are **mindful**, **honest**, **vulnerable**, and **genuine** in expressing themselves?

That's when we begin to see this medium transform into one that provides healing, growth, connection, understanding, empathy, and union.

My experience in the online eating disorder recovery community I found on Instagram years ago changed my life forever. I was broken and afraid of the unknown, and then, I stepped into a world of others who shared my feelings. I saw people going through it; I saw people who proved that you could make it out on the other side and be happy. I was given hope in vast amounts.

Here's how I got started.

My platform began as an anonymous food diary to hold myself accountable for my meal plan.

I remember the first picture I took—it was on a Saturday morning in the summer. My dad woke up early to water the garden. As I cooked breakfast, he entered the kitchen with the most breathtaking bundle of blue hydrangeas. We trimmed them and put them in a vase, then set them down on the table. I placed my breakfast in front of the vase. It was a piping hot plate of scrambled eggs and a perfectly toasted English muffin smeared with melted butter. I was afraid to eat, and my hands were shaking as I held up my phone to snap a photo. The flowers looked beautiful, and my dad smiled at me, and I felt a sudden, crippling need to share this moment.

I posted the photo on Instagram.

And that was my first post on @seekingstrongerwings.

Anonymity

When I first created my profile, I knew I was too fragile to fully own my space. In other words, I wanted to share my story, I *needed* to, but I wasn't ready to put a face to the name. This self-awareness helped me decide to keep my profile anonymous. No photos of me, no last name, no locations—nothing that would reveal my identity. Anonymity allowed the process of documenting to be intimate and the healing to be a bit less overwhelming.

Note: We are all at different stages of different journeys, and the above is just one example of that. I never anticipated my profile becoming anything more than what it was from day one, a space of accountability and support when I needed it most. Anonymously entering this online community was the most comfortable way for me to do so at the time. This might not be a protective measure you need to take, and that's fine too.

If you're not sure where you stand when creating your profile, I'd lean toward going anonymous. You can always take ownership of your content as you grow into it and become more confident in your online presence. We all progress at our own speed. No pressure.

Username

Once you decide how personal you want your account to be, it's time to choose a username. Before I set up my account, I spent time scrolling through existing accounts on Instagram. I specifically looked at ones in the same niche space I was planning to enter (in my case, eating disorder recovery). I found many of these users chose handles that reflected goals they're seeking to achieve, whether that be to recover, get stronger, gain weight, heal, find peace with food, achieve body acceptance, etc. I loved this approach because it gave me foresight and added to the accountability factor this space served for me. Almost like manifesting my goals.

As the screen flashed in front of my eyes, prompting me to enter a username, I asked myself what I needed from this space. And that's when my fingers typed *seekingstrongerwings*. What I needed more than anything was support—support that I could turn into strength. That's the goal I have kept in mind since day one. It's the one I still lean on to this day.

This section is all about becoming an active, impactful, and uplifting member of an online community. It's important to remember that you are more than your username, so don't worry about finding the perfect one right away. Others will come to know you as the content you create and share, the comments and support you provide, and the overall presence you build over time.

My best advice is to go with a username that reflects your goals for this account. Words like, "grows," "heals," "journey," and "progress" are great jumping-off points.

Profile Picture

Choosing a profile picture is a small detail—mine was a Tumblr image of a sunflower field for as long as I can remember. Simply choose an image you like. It doesn't have to be a big decision because you can change it whenever you want. Leaving it imageless can feel a bit distanced and impersonal, though, so I do recommend you add a visual for the profile picture.

Bio

If you're looking to connect with others on a genuine, heartfelt level, it's important to share some details about yourself. Usually, age, gender identity, and a first name are the most helpful. That said, feel free to use a nickname rather than your true first name if that makes you feel more comfortable. The help you are seeking is also nice to include in your bio, so others understand your struggle. I had "eating disorder recovery" in mine at the beginning, which made it easy for others in the same situation to identify with me and choose to connect.

If there's anything that makes your journey unique, include that too—just be mindful of others' sensitivity. I've seen accounts whose bios showcase details such as lowest weight or number of hospitalizations. While I encourage being honest and vulnerable, there's a fine line between what is healing to share and what is triggering for others. Be mindful of others and their headspaces.

As a rule of thumb, I'd steer clear of any number-based, body-related details about yourself in your bio (and in general, really). We have so much to connect through beyond what can be measured.

Now that your account is set up, more or less, let's explore how to best create content to share in building your support network. But before then, it's important to understand our triggers and what we want out of our social media experience.

· ·

When I first began using Instagram to heal, I was overwhelmed by the number of people I could follow. It truly felt endless, and this created a bit of pressure to follow nearly everyone.

Such a panic-driven state led me to follow plenty of accounts that proved to be triggering for me and my progress (though at the time, I convinced myself they were helping me). I wish I would have taken the time to know myself better before building the network of content I would be exposed to daily.

While I can't go back in time and walk myself through this exercise, I hope that some of you can complete it now. Take a few minutes to ask yourself what your triggers are—these could be about anything.

Write those down. Ask yourself, *what imagery and/or text would make me uncomfortable?*

_____

_____

_____

_____

_____

_____

_____

_____

_____

Another purposeful way to seek out content that
will serve you is to ask *what is my definition of health
now?* Understanding this vision will help you choose a
username that reflects this definition. It may even guide
the language you include in your bio.

_____

_____

_____

_____

_____

_____

_____

Chapter 11

Understanding Your Community

When I began my online journey, it didn't go as smoothly as I had hoped. I wasn't always a **conscious consumer**. I wasn't always in touch with my body and mind's true needs, my true health. As I learned to navigate the Instagram community, things got better. Eventually, I found my tribe.

It took some time for me to learn. I want you to avoid the pitfalls I ran into.

When it came to finding accounts to follow, all I knew was that I was looking to restore my "health." I took this word and ran with it. I followed plenty of eating disorder recovery accounts and even more accounts run by those who had come out on the other side. Both types of content were comforting for me to see, and I'm grateful I consumed each.

But I also followed personal trainers and fitness influencers. I filled my feed with exercise and told myself that I was using this content as motivation. I thought I too could work out when weight restored. In theory, that makes sense.

In reality, that wasn't the case. Each time I saw a workout video on my timeline, I subconsciously projected my situation onto it. Feelings of guilt and embarrassment would flood me. I would be eating my third snack of the day, bloated and uncomfortably full, watching burpee after burpee. I'd feel bad about myself for standing lazily on the sidelines.

I wasn't motivated by this content like I tried to convince myself—I was guilt-ridden and triggered.

My story is just one example. However, if you are using social media and online communities to heal, *be intentional about how you do*. The messages we are exposed to stick with us, whether we actively think about them or not. Every pushup that flashed before my eyes as I scrolled communicated a message to me.

The content we consume impacts us. This is why social media can be a toxic place. *It is also why social media can be deeply healing*. To do so, users must be deeply in touch with and honest about their own unique needs at the present moment.

Not everyone reading this will be creating an account to recover from an eating disorder. You may cultivate your own corner of the internet to navigate your relationship with your body image or even celebrate body positivity. While my story is the only story I can tell, I hope that in sharing it, you will find general guidance, insight, and advice to help you with your own social media use and experience going forward.

Ask yourself these questions: What will benefit me? What content will serve me? What content may trigger me so I can avoid it?

Consumer culture has led many of us to lose our sense of self. Taking charge of who you are and who you want to be is a self-reflective process. For the purposes of digging deeply into your sense of self, social media can be used as inspiration, but be sure to view it with a real-life filter. Keep in mind that people are presenting themselves and specific moments in their life on social media as they would like them to be, not necessarily as how their life always is. I gave an example earlier of the first Instagram photo I shared under my @seekingstrongerwings handle. I was inspired by the gorgeous flowers my dad brought in and placed on the table. It created a scene that isn't always a part of my morning. I don't have a photographic bunch of flowers on my table every time I sit down to eat. It was a picture-perfect moment. Remember that example as you view the scenes of life presented on social media. They are called "set up shots" because people have taken time to make the scene look ideal. It's not a true reflection of their everyday. Think of the photos as aspirational but don't allow them to make you feel *less than*.

Let's dive into some terms that bridge the gap between ourselves as individuals and the content we come across on social media.

Media Literacy

We live in a media-saturated world. From billboards to TV to social media, we are exposed to messaging every day. These messages come at us constantly. It can be overwhelming. As a result, we may feel burnt out trying to pay attention to each one. **Media literacy** calls for educating ourselves about how to *critically* consume content. It is about developing a *complete* understanding of messages so that the user can arrive at their own interpretations of each one. When we exercise media literacy, *we control* the messages we see, instead of *letting the messages control our thinking* for us.

Media literacy is a skill that can be developed by running through a series of questions each time you come across a message on social media that is attempting to make you think a certain way.

Asking these questions as I'm scrolling through Instagram is a habit I've forced myself to develop. As I'm consuming and engaging with content, I ask myself the following questions in this order:

1. **Who created this message/piece of content? What is their philosophy about the topic they're sharing? Do I align with this philosophy, and does it serve me?**

   Pay attention to the agenda of those sharing the content. Ask yourself who is behind it and what they are trying to accomplish by posting it. Almost all content has a perspective that influences the message, whether directly or in more subtle ways.

2. **What role does this content play in my life? Does it fit healthfully into my life at this time?**

   Actively thinking about how we plan to integrate the content into our lives allows us to take control. If we understand where the message is coming from, we can decide if we find it valuable or helpful or if we disagree with the message and find it to be possibly harmful. This step allows us to filter the information before it heads into our subconscious. If we disagree with the content creator's values, we can mindfully decide to move on without letting it take up a toxic place in our mind and subconsciously influence us.

Why it's important:

When we're using online communities to heal, there is great potential for comparison. One reason social media is often referred to as a "comparison trap" is that users fail to properly analyze and comprehend the content they see. We instantly project ourselves into the content we're shown.

When I first entered an online healing community, I constantly compared myself to others in an unhealthy and unproductive way. I would sift through others' meal journals and tell myself I was gathering inspiration. Really, I was looking to see if others were eating the same amount or more than me, and then using this information to validate my own meal plan.

Remembering habits like this makes me passionate about sharing tools such as media literacy today—it's a skill set I wish I had when I was more impressionable and more easily influenced by thousands of messages.

Maybe if I had taken the time to better analyze the content I was engaging with, especially the content that made me uncomfortable, I would have realized there was more to each message than what I saw on the surface. Media literacy helps us understand *how messages shape our world*. When we practice it on social media, this skill can show us *how content shapes our view of ourselves and the role we play in the world*.

Content has control over us when we passively allow it to live in our minds—whether consciously or subconsciously. When we *thoroughly think through* content, we *break it down* into parts that we can understand and see clearly.

We can see when and if we're being persuaded to think a certain way. We can see the creator's agenda and decide whether we agree with it or not.

Media literacy forces us to ask questions whose answers help us think for ourselves.

Using media literacy when interacting with content in online healing communities (and interacting with any online community) helps us better support ourselves and our needs.

So now that we understand *how* to healthily engage with messages we see, let's take it one step further. How do we go about *choosing* the content we want to see and engage?

As an extension, how do we do so in a way that *honors* and *protects* our well-being?

. . . .

As a consumer on social media, we are constantly inundated by content. So much so that it can be difficult to stay true to yourself when you're being shown thought-influencing content left and right.

Just log into Instagram and go to your Explore page, which is carefully curated to show you content that an algorithm has chosen. While the algorithm does take into account the type of material you've chosen to interact with in the past, it also chooses which posts pop into your feed, therefore influencing the content you interact with. It's an endless cycle. Is your head spinning? Same.

So, let's put the "conscious" in **conscious consumerism**. Being an active member of an online community means that you have the power to filter what you see. Think about it: when you choose what accounts you follow, you make a conscious choice to consume specific content.

Being a conscious consumer means that *you are aware of your needs as a user, and you then make informed decisions based on this self-reflective information.*

Examples of practicing conscious consumerism in online healing communities:

Example	How to
Following accounts and people that make you feel supported in your healing journey	When browsing accounts, poke through their in-feed content, stories, and profile highlights. Try to gather a good sense of overall life and wellness philosophies. *Does their content make you question the validity of your own choices? Do you find yourself comparing aspects of your life to theirs in a negative way?* Asking hard questions requires complete honesty. If you feel triggered by their content, then immediately unfollow them. Out of sight, out of mind.

Example	How to
Limiting and filtering what you see and adjusting these settings accordingly over time.	At the time of this writing, Instagram users have access to multiple tools to tailor their app experience to meet their needs. If you feel obligated to follow someone (maybe this person supports you, but their content is triggering for you to consume), you can mute their stories and/or feed posts. In other words, you can still be following them, but their content won't pop up on your timeline. I take advantage of both of these features. No guilt to be felt here. You're watching out for your own needs and providing love and support in a way that is mindful of your fragility. It's through healthy selfishness like this that we begin to heal and find our footing.

As we can see, **conscious consumerism** is all about being aware and informed. It's listening to our deepest selves and meeting ourselves where we are.

Chapter 12

Individualize

As we know (and I'll keep reminding us), true health is wonderfully individualized. It is a state of being that changes with us as we grow and explore new chapters of our lives. **It looks different for every single person.** It feels natural and peaceful. True health is the result of self-acceptance and self-respect. I find comfort in this. When I remember that my true health will never look exactly like anyone else's, I free myself from comparison and pressure.

Before following an intense meal plan, looking to restore weight, I was on total exercise restriction. These were goals I was struggling with and therefore needed support from others who understood *why* they were difficult for me.

Health, at that time, meant eating in a surplus with little movement and an abundance of genuine self-love and positive self-talk. If I had laid this definition out in front of me before diving headfirst into the online realm, I would have been able to easily identify my triggers. Back then, those would have been visuals like full-body images, workout routines, accounts that supported restrictive diets, and, of course, any pro-eating disorder content (this will always be hard to avoid entirely, as users behind these accounts will use hashtags and other tools to trick the app into looping them into pro-recovery content—this is an example of when media literacy is important).

By laying out exactly what I *didn't* want to see, I was able to filter through accounts and content that *did* serve me.

Healthy Consumer Habits

What determines how we experience online healing communities is the way we play our roles as consumers. We must be self-aware about our needs and take them into account. We must be sensitive to ourselves and to those around us. We must strive to uplift and improve and encourage and support.

How did I learn this?

By finally **unfollowing** the people that triggered me. It sounds simple, but it took me hurting repeatedly to connect the dots and then act on it. Self-advocating is incredibly hard.

I want to be clear that someone's content being triggering for me reflects **me** and **my** needs, not necessarily that person's intentions. In a full-circle moment, I went back years later and followed many of the accounts I originally unfollowed. It's funny how we grow into new selves, new needs, new definitions of health. There is beauty in flux, in the fusion of the "have been" and the "will become."

The hardest part about getting started as a consumer in an online healing community is finding accounts and content that **truly** serves you. One of the luxuries of controlling our own social media presence and landscape is that we can follow and unfollow new accounts any time we want—nothing is binding.

Once you've discovered spaces you find security and comfort in, it's time to build those healing relationships. When we use online communities to heal, we're looking for connection and shared experience.

We're looking for people who understand our pain. For people who appreciate how hard of a fight we're enduring to overcome hardships. For people who show us that we're not alone.

When we feel seen, we continue to reveal.

When I first entered this space, simply seeing others on this journey in real time was comforting. I watched from a distance as fighters compiled raw, honest stories. Some shared the challenges of weight gain. Others shared recovery wins. How did they challenge their disorders today? I was there for it all, immersing myself in a community filled with endless support.

For so long, I had suffered in isolated, unrelatable silence. Then I saw that I wasn't alone.

However, the accounts that helped me the most were not run by those *in* recovery but those who had made it beyond this point. They spoke about how the pain was worth it in the end, and they gave me hope for my future. I laid on my bed scrolling, and my skin felt a little tight on my body, and I was anxious about dinner, but then their posts popped up on my feed. I was reminded that they'd been here, right where I was, and they'd gotten out.

Angels. All of them.

This online Instagram community aided me in enduring the pain of recovery by giving me shoulders to rest my head on when it got hard.

Together we all fight.

One bite, one rest, one breath, one follow, one comment at a time.

It is a beautiful thing to work on our relationships with ourselves alongside other people—this is the magic of community.

Hashtags

I mentioned earlier that I accidentally stumbled upon the online eating disorder recovery community when I came across hashtags. Hashtags are an extremely powerful tool in pushing content to other users.

Just about anything can be hashtagged, so to start finding accounts you want to follow, I would pop a hashtag in front of keywords you're interested in. Some that I find useful are #_____recovery, #recoveryinspo, #healing, #bodyacceptance, #selflove, etc. You get the picture.

Anything that aligns with your definition of health is fully in play here. I tend to lean toward more positive and uplifting hashtags, as users hashtagging their photos with such words/phrases are often doing so with sensitive audience members in mind.

To give a more specific example of this thought process, here is a chart of hashtags that I would have avoided when I was looking to heal from an eating disorder in an online healing community (feel free to use these as a jumping-off point for your healing journey):

Hashtag	Reasoning
#weightloss	I don't find content about this process uplifting to *me*, given my history and self-love journey. If this is truly part of your definition of health at this time, maybe it's one you want to explore.
#proana, #proeatingdisorder, #probulimia	Anything that promotes the principles of the disorder I was healing from? No thanks.
#anorexia, #bulimia, #bingeeating, #eatingdisorder	Ah, these get tricky. Not all of the content attached to disorder hashtags will promote them. Many will be attached to recovery-based content and stories about overcoming such traumas. However, this content may be triggering and unpredictable since there's no bit about recovery included.

Hashtag	Reasoning
#fitness (and anything related to this term)	Here's a great example of why words related to health are *relative*. Terms like fitness, exercise, and movement are typically associated with good health and overall wellness. There's no arguing that. However, when I reflect on my past definition of health, I know I was looking to heal my relationship with compulsive exercise. To watch others work out when I desperately wanted to and couldn't would have been similar to a recovering alcoholic sitting in a bar.

Hindsight is 20/20. I learned through trial and error. I hope you don't have to—I hope these words reach and resonate with you, so you don't have to experience the same self-destructive practices I have in years past.

Chapter 13

Connecting Consumer

If you're a consumer looking to heal in online communities and have set up your profile and have begun finding content you align with, see yourself in, and can grow from, it's now time to start interacting with others.

You may be familiar with the term "ghost follower." If you're not, this refers to a user who only follows other accounts to silently view their content but doesn't post any of their own. While I believe you can benefit from engaging with healing content, you'll only find the *deepest* fulfillment when making those genuine connections with the people producing the content. I know it's scary to put yourself out there, but if there's any space to do it, it's online healing communities.

Just like our relationships in real life, the ones we develop online require attention and dedicated effort to be maintained. When I was sick, I isolated myself and refused to nurture the relationships in my life. I simply didn't have the will or energy. I stayed stuck for so long, and I was lonely.

In my online healing community, I found the potential to be understood. This gave me hope, which fueled my dedication to relationships I found online. What began as a comment here or there on someone's account grew into my genuine care for their well-being.

Connecting

As I mentioned before, I initially used my account as a food diary. I would post a photo of my meal or snack and use the caption as a diary.

Sometimes I was challenging myself with what I considered a "fear food" (a food I was afraid to eat for irrational reasons). I'd express my anxiety and how hard this moment was for me. I didn't know anyone who could relate to such suffocating fear when faced with a brownie after dinner, but I was beginning to realize that I wasn't alone in this online healing community. I expressed myself in hopes that others like me would see it.

And they did.

In the beginning, it was only one or two random strangers who, somehow, by the grace of hashtags, stumbled across my content. Even just one simple comment from a user I didn't know, such as, "You got this!" or "Rooting for you!" was all I needed in that moment of paralyzing fear. Their acknowledgment and encouragement made me feel obligated to eat.

And I did.

Not without great fear and difficulty, a bit of anxiety, and the occasional freak-out—but I felt accountability to those who had taken the time to encourage me, and so I soldiered on. And each post I shared and each follow, like, and comment my post received helped me begin to experience an internal shift.

As a consumer of others' content, it's extremely important to express support. **Following, liking, commenting, sharing**—taking time out of your day to build relationships is what makes online healing communities powerful.

I had half-heartedly tried to recover countless times. Each was marked by relapse. I kept slipping back into the comfort of my old, unhealthy behaviors because *I didn't see myself represented in the world around me.* This feeling of isolation made the burden of recovery too heavy to bear alone.

But the encouragement I received through my Instagram posts allowed me to feel *understanding* on a new level.

I felt safe professing my deepest, most irrational fears online because I believed that the audience it reached wouldn't judge me. I knew this because others in this space made sure I knew.

What a wild concept to be loved and supported so honestly, so consistently, by people I had never met and would likely never meet.

Okay, yes, I know what you're thinking: *Couldn't these people be faking?* How would I know who was genuine and who was not? We learn about catfishing and internet safety at a young age. With a topic as intimate and painful as eating disorders, though, it's truly hard for me to imagine that many people went out of their way to give me fake encouragement. That said, stay vigilant. If someone you only know through an online forum wants to meet in person, don't necessarily jump to trusting them. And if you do decide to get together, be sure to bring a friend and meet in a public place.

I truly don't think there are many disingenuous people in online healing communities, though. I say this because the connections I made and the stories I heard and the fears I related to were so real. Maybe I never experienced the same behaviors or beliefs as the people I came to know, but I was able to find bits and pieces of myself in their tales.

Community in Action

Here's a great example of me opening my heart and receiving love in return. On February 1, 2018, I posted a bowl of oatmeal with the following caption:

> "i can't believe it's already february. time is w i l d. here's a breakfast that's timeless: chia seed pudding oats 😋 can't go wrong with a classic! i've been having a really strong couple of days where i've felt just straight up happy and confident. today i woke up and was disappointed that i was a little sad. i felt like i had failed to keep such a good streak going. but i quickly realized that feelings are fleeting, and they're all valid. i can't blame myself for any feeling i have, positive or negative. what's important is that i recognize it, sit with it, and navigate it to the best of my ability. life's all about what works for YOU. gonna ride out this mini funk with some good food, a call to my mama, and a trip to the gym. sending you all love and the strength to push through to friday! we gotttttt this 💯"

Some of my favorite comments from this post:

> *"You are strong and can get through anything if you just keep fighting!!!"*
>
> *"that pool of nut butter 😋 hope you have a solid day today!!"*
>
> *"Best 🖤🖤 I SO get that! The good feelings come and go for sure. Sending you 💜💜"*

It only took a few minutes out of each person's day to like my photo and send these kind affirmations my way. That's it. How beautiful it is that our words can reach across borders and oceans in a matter of seconds? That they can find us when we need them most and prop us up, breathe fresh air into our tired lungs, and give us hope?

These people kept me going when I couldn't imagine holding myself up on my own. They showed me love. They consistently checked in. They cheered me on through my recovery wins and saw me through my steps backward. I came to know them as more than usernames and comments; we dedicated ourselves to each other's success and found friendship along the way.

I know firsthand how powerful the connections we find online can be. The love, peace, growth, and restored livelihood I have found in online healing communities are direct results of the genuine connections I've made as a connecting consumer.

Immersing yourself in these online healing communities doesn't have to be time-consuming. *Prioritize* connection the same way you prioritize things like work and sleep. My time spent on social media contributed directly to my health and wellness, so it was certainly worth my time. Even if it's only for a few minutes each day, be present in online spaces where others understand the pains you're facing.

It was therapeutic for me to use my space to serve my healing. Using the caption section to vent was cathartic. Taking photos of my food was exciting, sometimes even fun, and seeing the aesthetic of my feed overall caused me to start thinking like an artist. What next meal would complement the others? Even though eating was scary, something about curating a visual space of my meals provided a small love (oh, how this would grow) for adding new and different meals into my rotation.

It's now six years later, and I still wake up each day excited to see what my online friends are up to. I like to see how they are growing, creating, changing their lives, and changing mine. They begin difficult conversations, face their fears, take on challenges, and inspire the members of their own communities.

I feel honored to be welcomed into the life of another person on such an intimate level.

I feel empowered to keep supporting, keep seeing myself in other people, and keep learning from stories that are both like mine and those that are nothing like mine. I find security in both alike.

We grow together.

We're all here to be better, so go ahead and send a DM or leave a comment. You'll be amazed by the conversations that are out there waiting to be had, waiting to change your life. In small ways. In big ones.

When it comes to supporting others in these spaces, consistency is key. Healing from pains that have made our lives difficult can feel unstable—one day, we feel empowered and strong, the next hopeless and crippled with fear, so try to be supportive of those you follow regularly. They will be looking for your encouragement. It's fine to tell those who follow you that you want to hear from them, too.

My healing process called for challenging harmful beliefs and behaviors that I once found comfort in. Breaking routines, patterns, and schedules left me reaching for stabilizing factors in my life. *Consistent support from others grounded me.*

At a time when everything in my life felt like it was flipping upside down, the support I gave and received online kept my head above the water.

Here are some general guidelines to keep in mind:

Do	Don't
Use encouraging words and phrases with uplifting tones.	Be rude or put pressure on others. "You got this!" is different from "I was able to _____, why can't you?"
Be relatable—if someone posts about an experience that you can relate to, let them know they aren't alone.	Go into extreme detail, as this can be triggering. Hearing about specific behaviors won't serve this person and will only provide points of comparison for them to fixate over.
Offer to listen. Let them know your inbox is always open. When and if they feel ready, they'll know they can come to you.	Overstep. If you see someone is struggling, be gentle. Avoid judgment and "you" statements. Providing support is different from offering unsolicited advice/opinions.

Chapter 14

Producer Community

I spent nearly two years healing on Instagram, consuming content, contributing my own, and finding support. The more time I spent in this healing space, the more inspired I felt. A deep calling to do *more* spread through me like wildfire. During those two years, I worked diligently to mend my relationships with food, my body, and myself. I was still growing, still healing—but I was excited by how far I had come and the places I would continue to go.

I felt a calling to do more. A calling to share my story. A calling to produce.

Although I got off to a rocky start by following some Instagrammers whose feeds were triggering me, my plan from the beginning was to use Instagram to heal. I realized I had gradually become a producer, even though I wasn't yet comfortable sharing my true identity.

In the beginning, I was using my content as a means of cathartic release and accountability. But, after years immersed in an online healing community that continually showed me the value of genuine health, I felt ready to use my content as a means of inspiring hope in others. My goal became to show others that it *is* possible to find peace and happiness after pain. To show them what it looks like in real time and to help others understand what I had learned, which is that it's okay to be human in the process.

Somewhere along the way, I had gone from following a strict meal plan to falling in love with cooking, food, and nourishment. I had become a different person than I was when I first entered this online space. My transition from being a consumer to being someone who engages with others' posts *and* produces content reflects that growth.

I found strength in being vulnerable. When something is difficult to talk about, it means we should be talking about it. In online healing communities, talking is power. Opening conversations is power. Letting others into intimate corners of our pain is power because it allows us to bring this hurt out into the light and face it over and over again until it loses its power over us.

I learned this firsthand as a consumer. I watched others be vulnerable about sensitive topics and break down large barriers. I saw my pain reflected in thousands of stories that were hard to tell. The vulnerability of others lifted me and gave me hope.

My need to give back drove me to become a producer—and later, a thought leader—in an online healing community.

I didn't shed my need for consuming content. I'll always lean on the supportive, uplifting content of my fellow thought leaders. Being a producer in a healing community means *listening* above all else. To myself, to those around me. This insight helped me create content that allowed me to heal and allowed me to help others heal.

Taking the Leap

There are no rules for becoming a producer in an online healing community, and there is beauty in that freedom. We find ourselves when we have space to fill.

I'm no stranger to anxiety. Owning my space was scary in the beginning because I harbored a fear of being judged. I was still working through my recovery and, therefore, in need of constant support and connection. After two years of being part of an online healing community, I was in a place of good health with a goal to keep improving. I wanted to find even more balance, more peace, more freedom.

I became a producer not because I knew everything about what I was healing from and certainly not because I was 100 percent healed from it at all. I became a producer *because* I was healing currently, and sharing my story was deeply therapeutic.

All of this to say, don't second guess yourself. If you feel called to share your story, share it. Share it as the person you are right now, in this moment. You don't need to be healed to be here. You're here *because* you're healing. You can inspire, support, and uplift others while you're going through it yourself. We'll get into how to best do that in a bit.

Tapping into Mindful Authenticity

Authenticity is key. Transparency is key. That said, be careful about which personal details you share and which you keep to yourself. For example, don't ever share things like your address or other information that could put you at risk.

When I began truly sharing my story online, I had so much to learn about myself. I've undergone change after change over the years. I had found new passions, new ways of living, new beliefs and values. I went from being a high school senior, to a college student, to a college graduate. My audience has seen me through various chapters in my life. I have felt endlessly supported and loved throughout each step, and my gratitude knows no bounds.

So how did I cultivate such a loyal, supportive community?

I shared my life with transparency even though was initially intimidated by the thought of being judged. I was scared to share photos of myself or talk about the fears I had. But if my eating disorder taught me anything, it was that nothing changes in a comfort zone—the only way to overcome a fear is to face it head-on.

That's exactly what I did once I got comfortable with who I was becoming. I left my comfort zone of anonymity and began talking about myself in more detail. I faced the fear of judgment by simply accepting that I would deal with it when and if it came my way. Someone once told me that there's no point in worrying about something twice, and I now try to live out that mantra.

I leaned into the idea that, like every other person, I am wildly unique and radically individual—I chose to own who I was even before I was confident in it. This was uncomfortable until it wasn't. The more time I took to get to know myself and then share that self with the world, the more I grew to love that person and believe in her.

The whole point of entering an online healing community is finding connection, seeing yourself reflected, and feeling comforted and supported. What keeps people coming back to the healing community is that they are looking for more healing and growth. What your job is as a producer is to foster that sense of community.

. . . .

Do share your story and everything great about it. Share your story and everything hard about it. Above all, always be mindful of and clear with your audience.

Things to avoid:	Something to note:
Any content that you would find triggering as a consumer (think numerical values like weight, calories, etc.).	Whenever I create content to share, I always ask myself if this would serve me as a consumer. When in doubt, always assume your content is reaching your most sensitive audience members and create from there.
Falsely claiming to be an expert/ professional on the topic you're sharing about.	This is so important. Sharing your experience is one thing but claiming to be some expert on it is misleading (not to mention unethical). I always emphasize that anything I'm sharing is my experience and nothing more than that, just in case the audience is unclear.

Producing content in an online healing community is just another means of healing. Transitioning from

consumer to producer is simply a matter of feeling
ready to own your story. It doesn't necessarily mean
you have all the answers.

. . . .

Chapter 15

Content Confidence

If there is one question I get asked more than, "Recipe?" it's how to grow your online healing community.

The best answer I have is simply to start producing, and the rest will fall into place.

My intention for my online space has been the same since day one—it is an outlet for me to find support, connection, and free expression. I didn't enter this space as a creator, but it shaped me into one. I didn't enter this space with a voice of an influencer, but I found one as I grew and as I healed.

Analytics Fixation

Once you become a producer, it's incredibly easy to get caught up in analytics, such as follower count, number of likes, number of views, etc. You may feel tempted to post content that you believe will get your numbers up and give you a fast pass to popularity. Resist this temptation. Ground yourself in your intentions and call on them often.

Remember that you're engaging with social media to find a healing community. It shouldn't be a numbers game. The values that matter most in our healing journeys cannot be measured or contained within numerical values. You can't quantify things like gratitude, forgiveness, peace, grace, genuine friendship, and unwavering loyalty.

When getting started as a producer, it's important to keep this intention at the forefront of your mind. Above all else, this space is yours and should be used to help you on your healing journey. Your content should feel like a release, an exhale. Those who value your vulnerability and appreciate your authenticity will stay. Those who don't align with your content will find their support system elsewhere, and that's perfectly okay. As part of a supportive healing community, you will understand and respect this decision.

Keep doing you. Focus on yourself and produce content that brings you joy and helps you deepen your relationship with your health and wellness.

Content Creation

As for the more technical side of creating content as a producer, specifically on Instagram, visuals are important. Because Instagram is an image-heavy platform, the photos you use to build your platform should communicate the tone and energy of your space. Use this as a chance to tap into your creativity. What inspires you? Where do you find beauty? Capture these moments and use them as vehicles to express yourself.

I discovered during my healing journey that I find cooking extremely therapeutic. Being in the kitchen, experimenting with dishes and flavors, and seeing firsthand how nourishing my body allowed me to find health in all areas of my life allowed me to find a deep gratitude for food. Falling in love with food again led me to visually devote my healing space to food itself.

Ask yourself what visually symbolizes your healing journey and jump off from there. If you find your greatest passion in writing, create text posts of some of your work and build a feed from those. If you've found inner peace in traveling, share images of past trips and corners of the world in which you found pieces of yourself.

Your content should reflect you as a person.

Always keep this need for authenticity at the forefront—if your content is forced and not genuine, your audience can feel that. Plus, pumping out content just for the sake of getting likes/views certainly won't serve you in the end. Think of building your feed like collecting bits and pieces of your ideal vision board. You should never feel confined to only posting certain types of content. This is *your* space. Experiment.

I sometimes scroll through my feed simply because I love the way it looks. I'm proud of the content I captured. I feel connected to it. Each piece holds a bit of my heart. Each post acts as a voice for the thoughts and feelings I want to express to the world around me.

Allow yourself to feel pride in your feed. Creative expression is an unmatched tool when it comes to healing. I've found new amounts of self-confidence through building a feed of both images and text.

Your audience may be drawn in by what they can see right away, but what will keep them is the story you tell in your words and actions. Above all else, you're a human being, and *that* is what others in this online healing space want to know the most about.

- What are your dreams, beliefs, opinions, and experiences?
- What is daily life like for you?
- How do you pass the time?
- What are your hobbies?
- Use your captions to let your personality shine through.

Giving your audience visually stimulating and satisfying content is lovely (how many times have you swooned over the aesthetic appeal of someone else's feed?), but the true value of an online healing space comes from the philosophy you communicate through all avenues of content creation (in-feed posts, stories, highlights, reels, IGTVs, captions—the tools for creative expression are many).

In a beautifully full-circle moment, we return to a common theme that I've touched on throughout the book: how the messages we are exposed to online can shape our perspectives on the world, food, exercise, our bodies, and ourselves. As a producer, you have the gift of creating content and messaging that will influence others. With this comes great social responsibility. Remember that with every piece of content you create and share, whether that's a simple story frame or an extensive in-feed thread, you play a part in shaping minds. Someone else has allowed you to have a role in their healing journey. This is an honor. Be respectful and make sure you are encouraging body positivity and emotional health.

I know firsthand how easy it is to slip into the analytics fixation. As I mentioned before, when numbers and analytics and metrics are right under our noses, it's hard not to pay them mind.

Here's what I tell myself when I find I'm worried about superficial things:

▶ My **goal** in this space is to **heal** both myself and others. It is to find inspiration, hope, comfort, community. It is to build relationships. **It is to inspire and be inspired**.

▶ Growing my following and expanding my reach is nowhere near as important as my **health** and **well-being**. If worrying over metrics is causing me anxiety and stress, I am *not* healing.

▶ If I pump out content for the sake of simply getting likes/comments/views/followers, my audience will see right through this. I am *not* genuine. I am *not* prioritizing the audience I have **now** but rather am **fixating** on one I *don't* even have yet. I must be **present** at this moment and work from here.

Chapter 16

The Role of Others

It seems to me that we cannot heal in isolation. Online healing communities bring us together and give us a means of connecting with other people we otherwise may have never crossed paths with. How many beautiful stories I've heard, how many lives I've peaked into, how many philosophies and passions and traditions I've come to know, all through interacting with my audience. It's an education in and of itself. I learn about myself from others. I learn more about the world.

I took a lot of psychology courses in college. My professors always touched on the concept of **mirror neurons**, which are neurons in our brains that fire both when *we* perform a specific action and when we *observe* someone else performing that action. Mirror neurons allow us to learn through imitation. In other words, we can reflect the behaviors of others. We can see them and feel them as our own.

Why do I bring these up?

I believe that online healing communities are successful spaces because of mirror neurons. Seeing others heal helps us heal as well.

When we form these spaces online that are specifically focused on niche issues and topics, we can bring together thousands of people from all over the world and show each other our healing processes.

A spark of hope. Our mirror neurons firing.

Seeing others heal helps us heal. Showing others how we're healing helps us heal. Online healing communities help us *see*. They help us *share*. We can borrow strength from those around us until we're strong enough to give it back.

What a beautiful, endless cycle.

Listening to Your Audience

Community engagement is where producers form genuine connections with their consumers. When we take the time to listen to our audience, we hear their needs. We can ask ourselves where those needs fit into our story. Then we can produce content that will best serve and help heal.

Producers in online healing communities must give their consumers a voice. We've talked about media messaging at large, how it tends to be toxic to healthy thinking and living, and how industries can persuade consumers to think a certain way because they think on their audience's behalf. We spoke about tools like media literacy and conscious consumerism to help us take back our independent thought and control.

As producers managing online healing spaces, we can help this process. We can encourage consumers to engage directly with our messages. We can ask for their feedback, opinions, and advice. In this way, we help them consider the messages they see. We are showing them that they have control over what they believe in and that they have a say in whether they want to incorporate the information into their lives.

Someone is listening. Someone hears them.

Since we are also dedicating our space to sharing our story, beliefs, views, and values, we give our audience an understanding of the *who* behind each message we share. Consumers will be able to make connections between what we shared and why we might have chosen to do so.

Our goal as producers in online healing communities is to collaborate, connect, and coexist. Whatever we are healing from, we are actively doing it together.

Supporting Fellow Producers

The support we provide for our followers is of equal importance to the support we provide for our fellow producers and thought leaders in our space. There is no competition in healthy online healing communities. Our spaces, like our health, are wonderfully and uniquely our own. Concepts like creative expression and vulnerability can't be measured. Comparison will kill us if we let it creep in.

Lift others up. There is no one right way to heal. Allow yourself to be inspired by the content you see other producers sharing. Support them and their work. Connect through mutual support for the work other leaders are doing online to promote healing. You will most likely find deep friendships along the way.

Dealing with Comparison

It is incredibly easy to compare our own spaces to others. Who has more followers or gets more likes? Who is growing faster than we are or is more popular?

I didn't create my online healing community with a goal of growth. I never believed my account would draw in large numbers and high engagement. The growth was organic. It is the result of being vulnerable. Followers are drawn in when they can find themselves in the content. They stay when they are encouraged to be active members of the space and feel heard, seen, valued, appreciated, and loved.

Create a visually appealing space in which you share your story with pride and strength. Cultivate a space that is warm and inviting by being a grounding source of support for others. Engage, engage, engage. Support others who are working, like you, to change conversations and promote healing.

Always be sensitive to vulnerable users. Always err on the side of caution when sharing messages. Always disclose that these are experiences, not medical/expert advice.

Always prioritize your mental, physical, and emotional health.

You are here to heal too.

Some tips for cultivating an inviting, warm space online:

The action item:	What this tells your audience:
Share your story in however much detail you feel comfortable with. Be vulnerable. Talk about stuff that nobody else is talking about. Open up these conversations, even if you don't see anyone else doing it (*especially* if you don't see anyone else doing it). This means there's a need.	You're leading by example here. Readers will find comfort in your words, even if they can't relate to your specific situation directly. Over time, they will begin to see you normalizing vulnerability as a tool for growth and feel invited to undergo the same process.
Be *real*. Feeling burnt out? Take some time off. Having a difficult week? Remind your audience that this is normal (we're human!) and mention how you're healthfully coping with this. Embrace all emotions and life moments. Showcase the good and the bad.	How many times have you heard Instagram described as a "highlight reel"? This tendency for users to only post about and speak to pieces of their lives that are good leaves followers feeling like they simply don't measure up. Meanwhile, they're not getting the whole picture. When we break through this habit and embrace our humanity in its entirety, our audience feels relief. They feel safe and can relate. In turn, they feel like they can talk about their difficult weeks too.

Interact, engage, encourage. Take advantage of tools that allow for direct follower interaction. Post question submission boxes and polls to your stories. Tell stories in your captions and task your followers with sharing their own in the comments. Your content is a conversation, not a showcase.	Audience engagement is everything. As a producer, you have the power to start conversations in your space, but what if it's one-sided? Giving others a voice is the best thing we can do for our audience members.
Be reliable. Be consistent. You don't have to post every single or even multiple times a day, but show up for your audience often. If you need to take time away from this online space, let your followers know so they don't worry or wonder what is going on with you.	Healing is work that requires stability. When we are looking to heal, we're looking for roots and the ability to ground ourselves. Staying active in your space by consistently sharing some means of content tells your followers that you're here, you've shown up, you're continuing to show up, and they can reliably find you.

People are drawn to authenticity. Be honest, be true. We all struggle. This is a *healing* community, and everyone within it is looking to grow beyond the things that pain them.

Recovery from anything is never linear. Addressing this truth is refreshing for others to see. This feeling is what makes other people stick around. There's something about it that says, "We're all just doing our best so let's do it together." There is no competition or pressure or judgment when we're honest and open.

Recipes

While all recovery/mental health/self-growth content I produce is close to my heart, recipe development has become a core part of my life. Cooking and baking are now ways for me to express love for both myself and my loved ones.

Falling in love with these practices has allowed me to find peace around food. Seeing a recipe through from start to finish is a rush of empowerment. Fueling my body with foods it loves and craves is an expression of gratitude. Each meal I make reminds me that a mindful relationship with food is priceless and worth the world.

I reached this point by immersing myself in a community of people searching for the same healthy relationship with food or had already reached it and now preaching this philosophy. There is a certain comfort in watching another person express genuine balance in their diet and lifestyle. It's an "a-ha" moment, proof that food won't always control your life but instead can play a positive, nourishing role.

For so long, I felt trapped by food. I feared that if I didn't control it then it would control me. Diet culture emphasizes the need to "control" our intake and diet. This is praised and encouraged. It is seen as an act of power and diligence. Our relationship with food should not be based on control but rather on appreciation and respect. To nourish ourselves through food is to nourish not only our bodies but also our minds and spirits. To eat is to live in every way. To love food is to deeply feel the beauty of being alive.

As we know by now, food is more than just fuel. It is a celebration of life. It is a means of connection. It is tradition. It is memories in the making. Below are some of my most loved recipes on @healthfulradiance. From my table to yours, with love and gratitude.

Salted Peanut Butter Oatmeal Blondies

Ingredients:

- 1 cup coconut sugar
- 1 cup peanut butter
- splash of vanilla
- 1 cup oat flour
- ½ cup oats

- pinch of baking powder
- pinch of sea salt
- ½ cup almond milk
- optional:
  chocolate of choice

Using a hand mixer, blend the coconut sugar, peanut butter, and vanilla until moist crumbles form. In a separate bowl, whisk together the remaining ingredients except for the almond milk. Add the dry mixture on top of the wet, then mix again using the mixer on the lowest setting. Slowly add in ½ cup of almond milk until the mixture moistens and large clumps form. Add more milk if needed. Finally, stir chocolate chips (if using) and pour mixture into a parchment paper-lined brownie tin. Bake at 350°F for 30 minutes.

Creamy Red Yogurt Curry

Ingredients:

- 1 onion, diced
- 2 cups cashew milk
- 1 container nondairy yogurt
- ½ cup water
- 1 red bell pepper, diced
- 2 zucchinis, diced

- 1 cup broccoli florets
- 1 can rinsed and drained chickpeas
- 2 tbsp red curry paste
- curry powder, sea salt, cumin

In a stovetop pot, sauté the onion in a generous amount of avocado oil until soft and fragrant. Add the red curry paste and cook for another minute or two. Now, add the veggies, chickpeas, cashew milk, yogurt, and water. Add spices here to your liking but know that you can add more later too. Bring to a boil and then cook at a simmer for a half-hour with frequent stirring (it will reduce and get thick). Cook for 35 to 40 minutes and serve over grains of choice.

Beet Veggie Burgers

Ingredients:

- 2 tbsp ground flaxseed
- 2 tbsp water
- 1 cup diced beets
- 2 medium carrots
- 1 can rinsed and drained black beans
- 1 chopped onion
- 2 cloves of garlic
- ⅓ cup sunflower seeds
- pinch of sea salt
- pinch of cumin
- 2 tbsp coconut aminos (can sub soy sauce)

In a small bowl, make a flax egg by mixing 1 tbsp ground flax with 2.5 tbsp water. Let sit to thicken. While that's setting, add the beets, carrots, black beans, onion, and garlic to a food processor and pulse until finely chopped. Then add the sunflower seeds, spices, and aminos. Blend on high until a thick batter forms. Transfer to a bowl, cover, and place in the fridge to set for 1 to 2 hours. After that time, set oven to 400°F. Form the batter into four patties and place on a parchment paper-lined cookie sheet. Bake for 35 minutes, then flip and bake for another 25. I store these in the fridge, but they can also be frozen. To reheat, broil in the toaster oven/oven for a few minutes.

Loaded Green Goddess Bowls

(makes two bowls)

Ingredients:

- 1 cup cooked quinoa
- 2 cups kale
- ¼ cup olive oil
- 1 cup steamed broccoli
- Pinch of sea salt
- Pinch of garlic powder
- Avocado pea dip (recipe below)

Start by making the dip. To a blender, add:

- 1 cup frozen peas (steamed for 2 minutes in the microwave)
- 2 cloves of garlic
- 1 ripe avocado
- 2 tbsp tahini
- 1 tbsp olive oil
- 1 tbsp Dijon mustard
- Pinch of sea salt
- ¼ cup water

Once a thick mixture forms, place to the side. Prepare the kale by massaging it in olive oil, sea salt, and garlic powder for a few minutes or until broken down and softened. Assemble the bowls by laying the kale as the base, then the quinoa. Add the broccoli on top and finish with a generous dollop of the dip on top.

Vegan Edible Cookie Dough

Ingredients:

- 1 can rinsed and drained chickpeas
- ⅓ cup salted creamy peanut butter (can sub any seed butter here to make it allergy friendly)
- ⅓ cup maple syrup
- ⅓ cup + 2 tbsp coconut flour
- pinch of sea salt
- splash of vanilla

Blend everything in a blender or food processor until a thick, crumbly dough forms. Stir in chocolate chips of choice. Pinch some of the batter between your fingers—if it doesn't hold together, add a tbsp more coconut flour. Once it sticks, you're good to go. Roll into balls and place in the fridge for a half-hour to set.

About the Author

Angelina Caruso is a health and wellness blogger and advocate. A communication and culture major, she currently manages the social media brand and online community @healthfulradiance. Here, she shares recipes, promotes eating disorder recovery, and fosters a positive space for mental health. Angelina currently resides in New York City.

Mango Publishing, established in 2014, publishes an eclectic list of books by diverse authors—both new and established voices—on topics ranging from business, personal growth, women's empowerment, LGBTQ studies, health, and spirituality to history, popular culture, time management, decluttering, lifestyle, mental wellness, aging, and sustainable living. We were recently named 2019 *and* 2020's #1 fastest-growing independent publisher by *Publishers Weekly*. Our success is driven by our main goal, which is to publish high-quality books that will entertain readers as well as make a positive difference in their lives.

Our readers are our most important resource; we value your input, suggestions, and ideas. We'd love to hear from you—after all, we are publishing books for you!

Please stay in touch with us and follow us at:
Facebook: Mango Publishing
Twitter: @MangoPublishing
Instagram: @MangoPublishing
LinkedIn: Mango Publishing
Pinterest: Mango Publishing
Newsletter: mangopublishinggroup.com/newsletter

Join us on Mango's journey to reinvent publishing, one book at a time.

CPSIA information can be obtained
at www.ICGtesting.com
Printed in the USA
JSHW041724180921
18761JS00005B/7